A Simple Guide To
CAKE DECORATING

Pam Leman and Maureen Gates

GP

ACKNOWLEDGEMENTS

We would like to thank Lyn Jelercic, Marilyn Lock, Denise Fuhrmann and Barbara Lumsden for their valuable assistance in the preparation of this book.
     We also extend our sincere gratitude to AUSTRALIAN BAKELS PTY LTD for donating the plastic icing used in this book.

Parafilm®: Trade name for plastic florist tape

First published 1989 by Golden Press Pty Ltd
Incorporated in NSW
46 Egerton Street, Silverwater, NSW, 2141

National Library of Australia
Cataloguing-in-Publication data

Leman, Pam.
   A simple guide to cake decorating.

   ISBN 0 7302 0599 1
   1. Cake decorating. I. Gates, Maureen. II. Title.

641.8'653

Printed In Singapore Through
Imago Productions (FE) Pte Ltd

Typeset in 10 pt Bembo by Deblaere Typesetters

Photography by David Levin   Sketches by Michelle McGarrigle
              William Rolan   Pam Leman
              Quentin Bacon   Shirley Peters
              Ray Joyce

FOREWORD

We have written this book to encourage and help those interested in Cake Decorating for that Special Occasion, yet not always able to attend classes. It is a good step by step reference book at an affordable price.

With practice and by following the simple instructions, a far more positive approach to Cake Decorating will be achieved by the student and the more experienced decorator.

We feel very confident it will be of great enjoyment and help to many.

Pam and Maureen

CONTENTS

ESSENTIAL EQUIPMENT

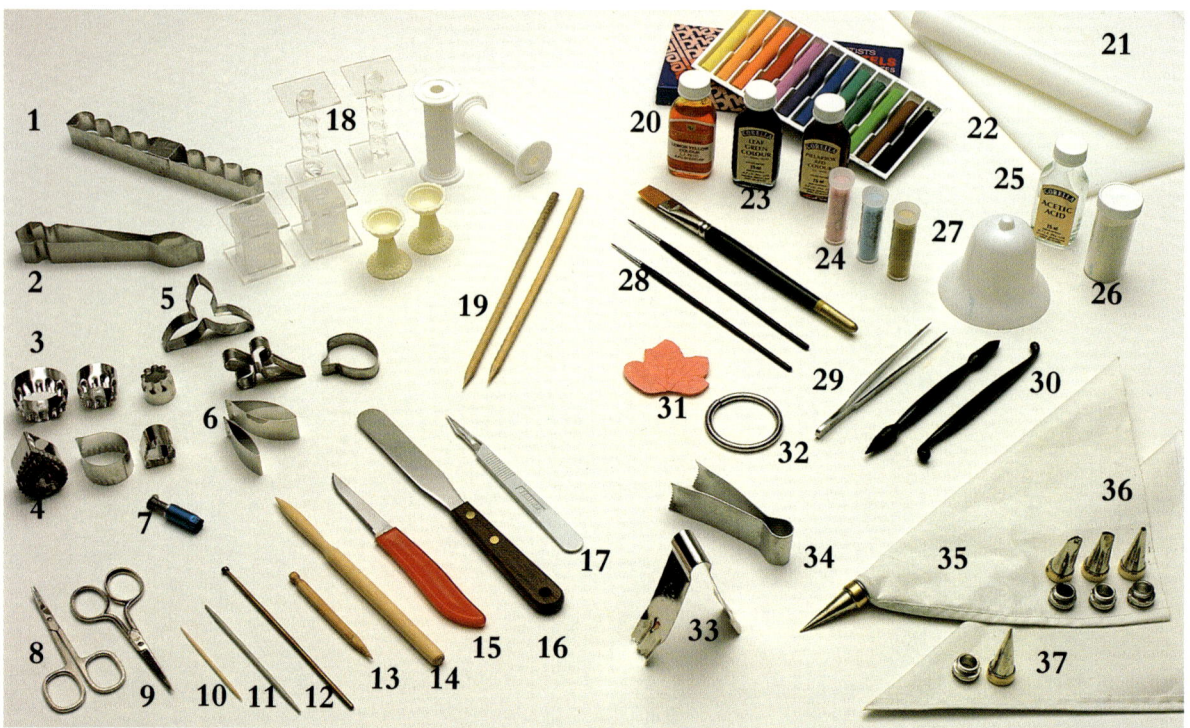

1. Straight frill cutter A tool used to make a Garrett frill in plastic icing along the base of a cake.

2. Fan cutter Used to form a fan in modelling paste.

3. Rose cutters Cutters in various sizes used to make a moulded or briar rose.

4. Rose leaf cutters Serrated-edged cutters used in conjunction with the rose cutters to make rose leaves.

5. Phalaenopsis orchid cutters These include a three-petal cutter, a 'wing' and a 'throat' of the phalaenopsis orchid.

6. Petal cutters Used to make a tiger lily or for the wings or sepals of cymbidium orchids.

7. Plunger cutter A simple cutter used to make forget-me-not flowers.

8. Curved scissors Used to cut curved petals when moulding very small petals, e.g. bouvardia or hyacinths.

9. Straight scissors Used to make straight cuts when moulding the centres of small flowers.

10. Toothpick An inexpensive tool used extensively in cake decorating for such things as hollowing out flowers or frilling an edge.

11. Cable knitting needle Also used to hollow out small flowers.

12. Ball tool A stainless steel ball-bearing soldered onto a handle, used to thin and shape flower petals. These can be purchased at leathercraft shops.

13. Wooden modelling tool (small-pointed) Used to hollow out larger flowers, e.g. Christmas bells.

14. Wooden modelling tool (long-pointed) Used to hollow out large flowers or to make a Garrett frill.

15. Sharp vegetable knife Used to make small cuts for inserted ribbon or to cut around plaques, etc.

16. Wooden-handled spatula
Used to cut the sides of a cake when icing with plastic fondant, or to smooth the base of a cake.

17 Scalpel Used in cake decorating to cut flowers or shapes out of modelling paste. These can be purchased at art supply shops.

18. Various pillars These are used to support tiered cakes. They come in various colours and sizes.

19. Wooden skewers These are placed into the cake in conjunction with pillars to support tiered cakes.

20. Non-toxic pastels (chalks) Used to colour moulded flowers made in sugar.

21. Rolling pin (small) Non-stick, used to roll out the modelling paste to make moulded flowers and plaques.

22. Board Non-stick, used with the rolling pin for thinly rolling out modelling paste.

23. Food colours – liquid Food colours are used to colour the modelling paste or icing.

24. Food colours – petal dust This is used as a colour to highlight flowers and give them a gloss.

25. Acetic acid An ingredient used as a drying agent in royal icing. It helps to dry lace etc. quickly.

26. Gum tragacanth Used when making the South African modelling paste.

27. Bell mould Used to make bells in modelling paste.

28. Paintbrushes Large brushes, sable or synthetic, are used to colour flowers when using non-toxic chalks.

Small brushes, Nos 00 and 0, are used to paint on fine details or to attach petals to the flowers.

29. Tweezers Long-pointed tweezers are used extensively in cake decorating for such jobs as placing stamens in the centre of the flowers.

30. Black modelling tools Formers (four and five-petal flowers) are used to mark veins or grooves in the centre of small flowers such as gypsophila.

'Dog Bones' are used to thin the outside edge of the petals.

31. Pink leaf mould Used for veining various wide leaves, e.g. violets.

32. Macrame ring Used with foil to give a base for moulded open rose petals when attaching them.

33. Crimper – large-toothed Used to make a pattern onto the cake.

34. Crimper – fine-toothed A curve-shaped crimper used also to make designs on the cake.

35. Complete piping bag, screw and writing tube Assembled ready to pipe with royal icing.

36. Extra tubes and screws These are essential when attaching the icing bag. The tubes include a star, leaf, petal and a writing tube, some of the most commonly used tubes in cake decorating.

37. Piping bag Used with screw and writing tubes in pipework.

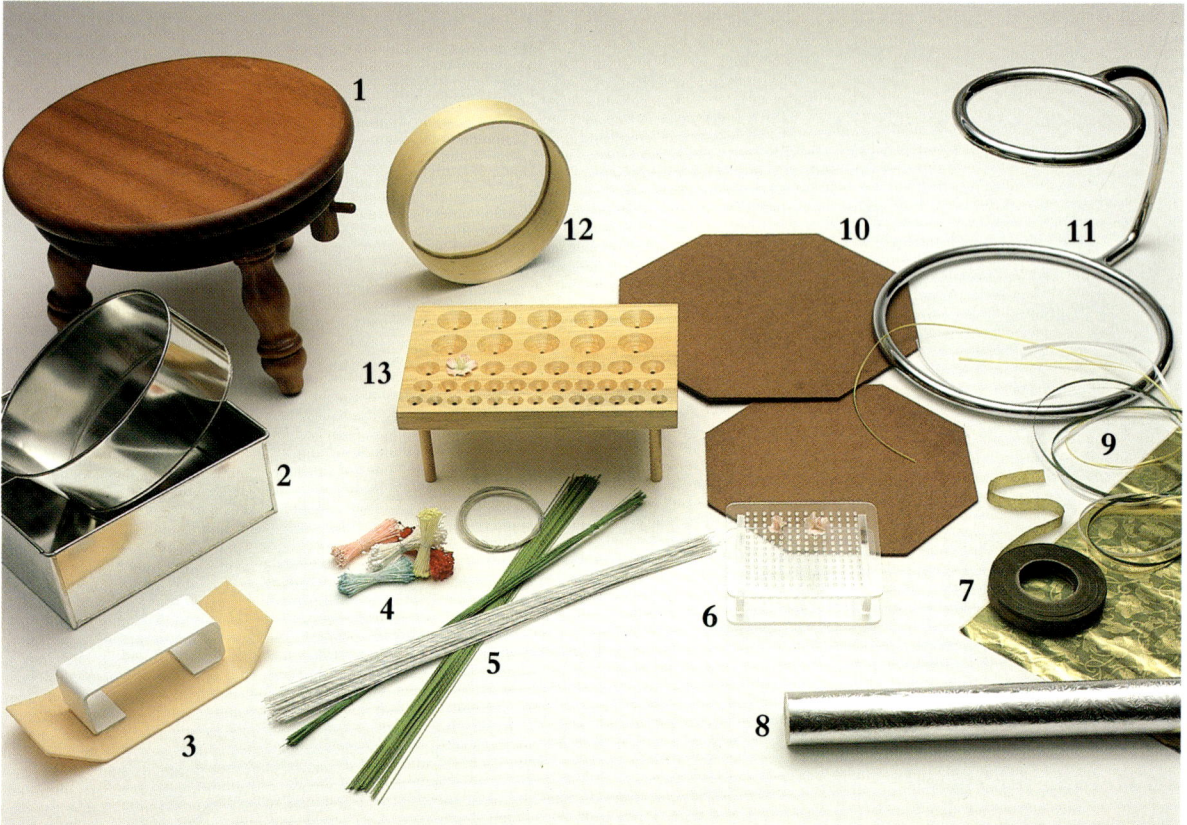

1. Wooden turntable Used to rest the cake on when decorating.

2. Cake tins Specialty cake tins suitable for decorated cakes are available in various shapes and sizes.

3. Smoother A handy tool used to achieve a smooth edge when icing a cake.

4. Stamens These are used in the centre of flowers – they come in various colours and sizes.

5. Wires Silk and paper-covered wires in green and white are suitable for making small flowers on.

6. Plastic holder with small holes Small moulded flowers are placed in these to dry.

7. Florist tape For wired sprays.

8. Paper Silver and gold paper is suitable for covering masonite boards.

9. Ribbons Fine ribbons are used for decorating cakes. Satin rayon ribbons are the best because they hold their shape when looped into bows.

10. Masonite boards Eight-sided boards suitable for similar-shaped cakes. Cake boards come in various shapes and sizes and

are available at leading cake decorating suppliers.

11. Cake stand A special stand, often shown in South African and British cake decorating books, to support tiered cakes.

12. Sieve This is one of the most essential tools for cake decorating. It is important to use a fine sieve when sifting pure icing sugar to make royal icing for pipework.

13. Flower holder Flowers can be assembled in this. The calyx is made and placed in the holder, the petals are attached to this and left in the holder to dry.

Equipment shown in these photographs came from A & J Cake Decorating Supplies, 16 Boyle Street, Sutherland, NSW.

RECIPES

Fruit Cake

INGREDIENTS
- 1.5 kg (3½ lb) mixed dried fruit
- 3 tablespoons rum
- 250 g (½ lb) butter
- 250 g (½ lb) sugar
- 2 heaped teaspoons marmalade
- 1 teaspoon vanilla essence
- 1 teaspoon almond essence
- 1 teaspoon Parisian essence
- 250 g (½ lb) plain flour
- 60 g (2 oz) self raising flour
- pinch salt
- 1 teaspoon cinnamon
- 2 teaspoons mixed spice
- 5 eggs
- 1 teaspoon glycerine

METHOD
Pour rum over fruit, stand overnight.

Cream butter and sugar, add marmalade and essences. Sieve the flour with the salt and spices and combine with the mixed fruit until the fruit is coated with the flour.

Add the eggs, one at a time to the butter and sugar mixture, beating well after each egg is added. Add half the fruit and flour mixture. Blend it in then combine with the other half until all the fruit is blended through, mix in the glycerine and place it in a greaseproof-lined tin. Bake at 140°C (275°F) for 3½-4 hours.

Note: This will fit into a 23 cm (9 in) size tin. When cooking the cake place a small pyrex dish of water in the oven, taking it out just before the cake is cooked to allow it to develop a crust.

Modelling Paste

INGREDIENTS

- 185 g (6 oz) pure icing sugar, sieved
- 2 teaspoons liquid glucose
- 2 scant teaspoons gelatine
- 1 tablespoon water
- 90–125 g (3-4 oz) extra pure icing sugar, sieved

METHOD

Sieve pure icing sugar, and place into a small pyrex bowl, cover with plastic food wrap until ready for use. Stand the bottle of liquid glucose in hot water for 5 minutes.

Bring water to be used to the boil.

Sprinkle into a small pyrex bowl 2 teaspoons of gelatine and 1 tablespoon of cold water.

Stand this mixture in a saucepan, slowly bringing it to the boil, allowing the water to come approximately halfway up the side of the bowl.

When the gelatine is dissolved, use a hot teaspoon to take the glucose and add it to the gelatine mixture, stir until dissolved (remove from stove for this process). Allow the mixture to become tepid. Make a well in the centre of the sieved icing sugar and add the warm liquid. Take a wooden spoon and draw the mixture away from the sides until the mixture is too difficult to handle any more.

Take the extra sieved icing sugar and place it onto a clean laminated board. Remove the icing sugar mixture from the bowl and add it to the extra icing sugar. Knead this until the mixture becomes non-tacky. Cover the modelling paste with plastic wrap and seal it in an airtight container, allow time for the paste to set before use.

Royal Icing

INGREDIENTS

- 1 egg white (room temperature)
- 315–375 g (12-13 oz) pure icing sugar, sieved
- 2 drops acetic acid (strength 60%)

METHOD

Place the egg white into a glass mixing bowl and, with a clean wooden spoon, lightly beat it for several minutes. Add a teaspoon of the sieved pure icing sugar and mix until it is thoroughly combined with the egg white.

Gradually beat in the icing sugar a tablespoon at a time, until the icing begins to thicken. Add 1-2 drops of acetic acid and reduce the sugar to a teaspoon at a time, until the icing is smooth and light and stands up in soft peaks. This procedure will take approximately 15-20 minutes. The icing should be white when completed. Place in an airtight container.

There are three consistencies:

'Soft-peak' consistency; when the wooden spoon is

drawn away from the icing mixture, it should fall slightly to the side, then hold a peak. This is used for pipework and embroidery, etc.

'Medium-peak' consistency; obtained by adding 1-2 teaspoonfuls of pure icing sugar to soft-peak royal icing. This is used for dropped thread and lace.

'Firm-peak' consistency; achieved by the addition of 1-2 dessertspoons of pure icing sugar to soft-peak royal icing. If the consistency is correct the icing should hold a firm peak. This is used for borders on cakes, lattice work etc.

'Sugar'; a sign that too much icing has been added, add a little egg white or lemon juice to bring the icing back to the correct consistency, beat well.

Marzipan or Almond Icing

METHOD

Sift the pure icing sugar and place into a clean glass bowl. Add marzipan meal or ground almonds and thoroughly combine the two ingredients.

Beat lightly the egg yolks, sweet sherry, lemon juice, glycerine and almond essence in a small separate bowl. Make a well in the centre of the dry ingredients and add this liquid. Turn the dough out onto a laminated surface which has been dusted lightly with pure sieved icing sugar. Knead until firm (the same consistency as shortcrust pastry).

If the paste is too short, add more lemon juice. If it is too wet, add extra sieved pure icing sugar.

Place in an airtight container.

Note: Manufactured marzipan can be purchased from cake decorating shops, supermarkets and delicatessens.

INGREDIENTS

- 500 g (1 lb) pure icing sugar, sieved
- 125 g (¼ lb) marzipan meal or ground almonds
- 2 egg yolks
- 1-2 tablespoons sweet sherry
- 2 tablespoons lemon juice, strained
- 1 tablepoon glycerine
- 1 drop almond essence
- extra pure icing sugar, sieved
- airtight plastic container

Plastic Icing

INGREDIENTS

- 750 g (1½ lb) pure icing sugar, sieved
- 3-4 tablespoons liquid glucose
- 6 teaspoons glycerine
- ¼ cup (60 ml) water
- 1 tablespoon gelatine
- 250 g (½ lb) extra pure icing sugar, sieved

METHOD

Sieve the pure icing sugar into a glass mixing bowl.

Measure out liquid ingredients in a measuring glass. Put the water into a small pyrex mixing bowl and stand the latter in a small saucepan and water. Sprinkle the gelatine over the water and heat it until all the gelatine is dissolved.

Take the mixture from the stove, leave it in the saucepan and put the glucose and glycerine into it.

Stir until they are well combined and fully dissolved. Allow this to reach room temperature, but do not wait until it is cold.

Make a well in the centre of the pure icing sugar and pour the tepid liquid into it. Using a wooden spoon or plastic spatula, start to bring in the icing sugar (similar to making pancake batter) until the mixture becomes difficult to manage without placing the hands into it. At this stage take the mixture out onto a clean laminated surface, sprinkled with sieved icing sugar, and knead the mixture into a workable dough.

Do not allow any dry crusty pieces of icing sugar to be taken into the fondant.

Place the icing, which has been wrapped in plastic, into an airtight container. When ready to use, add the extra sugar and knead the icing lightly with the palm of the hands – never the fingers, as this adds air bubbles to the icing.

Place into an airtight container.

PREPARING A CAKE TIN

STEP 1

Cut two pieces of greaseproof paper, the same shape as but slightly smaller than the base of the tin.

Cut also a double sheet of greaseproof paper, slightly longer than the circumference of the cake and 2.5 cm (1 in) taller than the height of the tin.

Fold the paper over about 2.5 cm (1 in) using sharp scissors make small cuts all along the length of the paper.

STEP 2

Place the long strips of greaseproof paper into the inside of the tin, making sure the paper takes the shape by pushing the paper firmly against the side of the tin, leaving an overlap of 2.5 cm (1 in) where the two pieces meet.

STEP 3

To complete, place the two remaining circular pieces of greaseproof paper into the base of the tin.

PLASTIC ICING LESSON
How to Pack a Cake

If the cake is not even, cut off the top and place the cake face down onto the plastic place mat. This creates a level surface to work on.

Fill any crease marks, gaps or holes with marzipan, almond or plastic icing. Roll out a small sausage of plastic icing and fill in around the base of the cake, making sure that the plastic icing is kept in alignment with the side of the cake. Press firmly against the cake with a spatula or flat knife so that no ridges or bumps show. Neaten off any excess plastic icing or marzipan with a sharp knife. Clean off excess cake crumbs before continuing.

Note: When using marzipan, almond or plastic icing keep airtight when not in use.

How to Ice a Cake

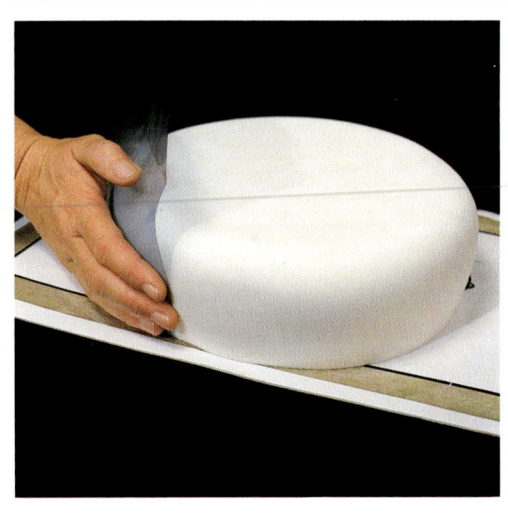

STEP 1

After making the required quantity of rolled fondant, knead the fondant with a little sieved icing sugar or cornflour. Using a clean bench, roll out the fondant with a large piece of conduit or a rolling pin, placing a small amount of cornflour under the icing while rolling it out to prevent it from sticking to the bench, when the icing is about 1 cm thick and approximately the size of the cake, measure it to see it is the correct size, pick up the fondant on a rolling pin and place it gently onto the cake, measure it to see it is the correct size, pick up the fondant on a rolling pin and place it gently onto the cake, do not allow excessive amounts of fondant to hang over the sides as its weight when attached will cause hairline cracks to form. Brush the cake lightly with boiled jam or egg white and attach the fondant to it.

Cup the corners, using the palm of the hand to rub backwards and forwards to secure the fondant against the side of the cake.

Press the fondant firmly against the base of the cake before cutting off any excess fondant with a sharp knife. Use a wooden plane, rub the top of the cake until smooth.

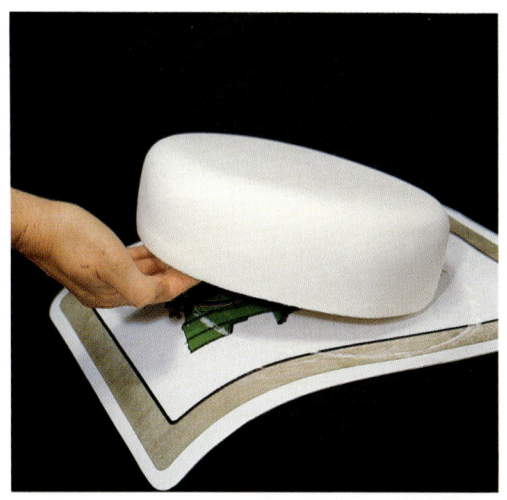

STEP 2

If hairline cracks appear around the top edge of the cake, quickly cut off the excess fondant at the base and bring the plastic acetate film up the side of the cake instead of down as usual, this will eliminate a lot of the cracks. Prick any air bubbles. Rub the acetate gently around the side of the cake to finish off the cover, again cut off any excess fondant around the base. Bring the place mat on which the cake is standing over to the side of the bench and release each side by pulling the mat downwards. Place your hand under the cake and lift it off the plastic mat ready to place onto the board.

STEP 3

Place a small amount of royal icing into the centre of the board, place the cake onto this and secure it, take a damp cloth and neaten the board if necessary.

WEDDING CAKES
Step by Step Preparation

TO PREPARE A CAKE BEFORE ICING

1. Cut a piece of masonite the same shape as the cake. Do not use cardboard, as it will not take the weight of the cake. **2.** Cut out a piece of silver or gold paper 1 cm (½ in) larger than the board. Apply paste or wood glue onto the board, spread it out evenly and cover the board with the paper. Use a damp tea towel to smooth out any air bubbles. Place a little more glue onto the sides of the board and, using damp tea towel, pull the paper firmly against the sides and fold over onto the back of the board. Cut another piece of paper, a little smaller than the first piece and glue it to the back.

3. Attach two wooden runners onto the base of the board to make the cake easier to pick up. If the board is for the top or second tier of a tiered cake, there is no need for runners.

4. If the cake is not even, cut off the top and place the cake face-down on a plastic place mat. You will now have a level surface to work on.

5. Fill any crease marks, gaps or holes with fondant or marzipan. Roll out a small 'sausage' of fondant and fill in the base of the cake, making sure that the fondant is kept in alignment with the sides of the cake. Press firmly against the cake with a spatula or flat knife so that no ridges or bumps show. Neaten off any excess fondant or marzipan with a sharp knife. Clean off any excess cake crumbs before continuing.

6. Before covering the cake with fondant or marzipan, use a pastry brush to apply egg white or boiled and strained jam to the surface of the cake. Use it sparingly. If marzipan paste is to be applied before the fondant, leave the marzipan for several days to allow it to dry out.

TO COVER A CAKE

1. Knead the fondant with a little sieved icing sugar.

2. Using a clean bench, roll out the fondant with a rolling pin, placing a little cornflour under the fondant while rolling it out to prevent it from sticking to the bench. When the fondant is about 1 cm thick, and approximately the size of the cake, place it on the cake. Do not make it so big that excessive amounts hang over the sides, as its weight when attached will cause hairline cracks to form.

3. After checking that the fondant is the right size, remove it from the cake and brush the cake with boiled sieved jam or egg white.

4. Pick up the fondant on a rolling pin and place it gently onto the cake. Sprinkle a little sieved icing sugar on your hands and smooth over the top of the cake with the palm of the hand to eliminate air bubbles, then secure the fondant to the sides of the cake.

5. Rub the palm of your hand backwards and forwards against the top edge of the cake to attach the fondant securely to the cake. Press the fondant firmly against the

GREASEPROOF TEMPLATE

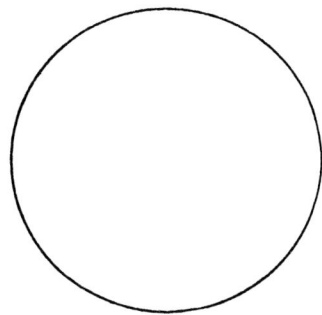

Greaseproof-paper template of the base board for the top tier

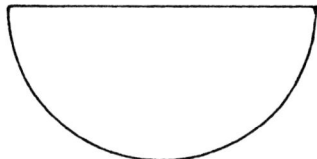

Template folded in half

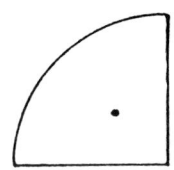

Folded in half again. Mark where the skewers will sit on the cake

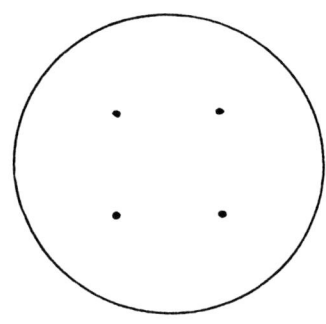

Push the skewers into the cake

base of the cake before cutting off any excess fondant with a clean sharp knife. Use a wooden plane or a piece of plastic acetate film to smooth the sides and top of the cake. (If hairline cracks appear at the top of the cake, quickly cut off the excess fondant and bring the plastic film up the sides of the cake instead of down as usual; this should eliminate a lot of the cracks.) Prick any air bubbles.

6. If the weather is windy, it is advisable to wait until the wind dies down before icing, or the cake may dry out too quickly.

7. Bring the place mat on which the cake is resting over to the side of the bench and release each side by pulling the mat downwards. Place your hand under the cake, and after attaching a small piece of royal icing onto the board, secure the cake in the centre.

8. If the cake is very large or is an irregular shape, it is easier to ice it straight onto the board, with a piece of waxed paper attached with egg white to the board. This will keep the board clean and can be cut away when the cake is complete.

THE PLACEMENT OF PILLARS ON A TIERED CAKE

You will need:
- wooden meat skewers
- pillars
- greaseproof-paper template of top tier base board

METHOD

1. Make a greaseproof-paper template of the base board for the top tier. Fold it in half, then in half again. Place a skewer through the four pieces of paper (see diagram).

2. Place the template in the centre of the bottom tier. Position the pillars onto the paper.

3. Insert the wooden skewers into the cake, then pull them back out and turn them over so that the point is facing upwards.

4. Replace the skewers into the cake and this time, using a pen, mark the skewers just above the point where the top of the pillar reaches. Remove them from the cake.

5. Cut off the skewers at the places marked. Remove the greaseproof template and insert the skewers back through the pillars and into the cakes.

6. When this process is completed, the weight of the cake should be on the wooden skewers – not on the pillars, which are normally of a fairly flimsy construction.

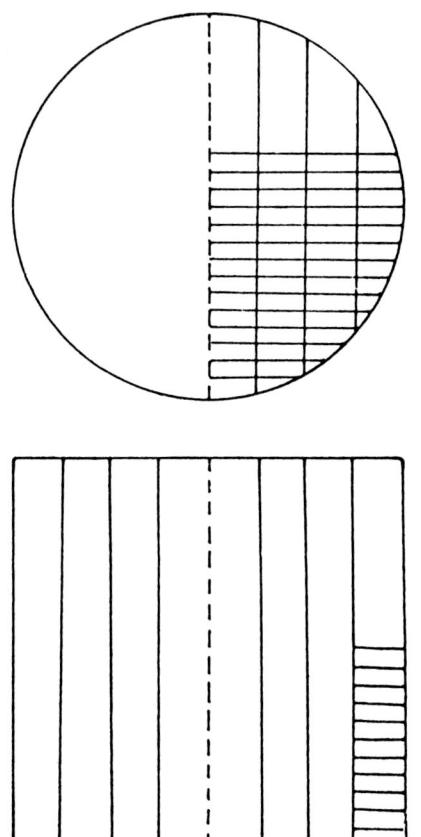

TO CUT A WEDDING CAKE

The first cut, or ceremonial cut, should be from the centre of the cake to the edge and then down to the board. The cake is then usually removed to the kitchen, where it is cut into pieces for the guests. Use an extremely sharp knife with a 25–30 cm blade. Never attempt to cut wedges, cut the cake in half, and then into slices. Cut each slice into pieces, according to how many guests you are serving.

TO KEEP THE TOP TIER OF A WEDDING CAKE

It is traditional for the bride to keep the top tier of her cake for 12 months. The best way to do this is to place it in an airtight plastic container and freeze it. Defrost it with the lid on, and even after 12 months, it will be in good condition.

FRESH FLOWERS
Spray for Top Tier of Cake

STEP 1

Using 26 gauge wire and the hairpin method wire small sprays of freesia buds. Apply Parafilm®.

Using 28 gauge wire and the hairpin method pass the wire through the base of the freesia bud. Apply Parafilm®.

Using fuse wire, form a hook and bring it firmly through the centre of the Roman hyacinth. Apply Parafilm®.

Using 26 gauge wire, form a hook and bring it firmly through the centre of the Dutch hyacinth. Apply Parafilm®.

Using 26 gauge wire the hairpin method wire asparagus plumosus. Apply Parafilm®.

REQUIREMENTS

- 5 sprays of small freesia buds
- 8 medium size freesia buds
- 17 Roman hyacinths
- 5 Dutch hyacinths
- 5 small pieces of asparagus plumosus
- fuse wire
- 28 gauge wire (0.38 mm)
- 26 gauge wire (0.46 mm)
- Parafilm®, green
- scissors and secateurs

STEP 2

Place five pieces of asparagus plumosus fern from a central point to form a circle and base for the spray.

Extend and place five sprays of small freesia buds. These should be evenly spaced from a central point and slightly elevated to form a circle.

Alternate and extend five freesia buds a fraction higher and slightly shorter than the sprays of small buds still coming from a central point. Squeeze the stems firmly together. Apply Parafilm®. Place three freesia buds in a vertical position, a bud slightly higher than the other two, all placed evenly around in a circle.

STEP 3

Position five Dutch hyacinths around the outside circle between the freesia buds still coming from a central point. Introduce the Roman hyacinth around the outside circle and into the spray to hide any gaps in your work.

Cut off any excess wire and squeeze the stems firmly together, applying Parafilm® to the remaining main stem.

Note: If you do not want to insert the wires into the cake, shorten the handle and attach the spray to a wooden skewer.

Spray for Bottom Tier of Cake

The trail has been divided into 4 equal sections. The flowers and ferns listed
are for one section of the trail.

REQUIREMENTS
- 5 sprays of small freesia buds
- 5 medium size freesia buds
- 5 freesias
- 25 Roman hyacinths
- 7 Dutch hyacinths
- 3 small pieces of asparagus plumosus
- fuse wire
- 28 gauge wire (0.38 mm)
- 26 gauge wire (0.46 mm)
- 22 gauge wire (0.71 mm)

STEP 1
Prepare the fern and flowers with suitable wire and
Parafilm® as described in top tier.

STEP 2
Measure the base of the cake and allow an additional
2.5 cm (1 in) in the length.

Join two 22 gauge wires together to obtain the length
measured in the previous step Parafilm® stretching the
tape until it is very thin and placing it firmly around the
wires.

Form a closed hook at one end of this piece of wire,
make a hook at the other end but leave it open until the
flowers have been assembled.

Work out the number of flowers to be used in a uniform
and evenly balanced trail, suitable for a repetitive design
to be placed along the full length of the circlet.

STEP 3
Place the freesias to the centre and to the left and right of
the centre wire, elevate these so that they do not rest on
the main stem, introduce small clusters of hyacinths
between the focal flowers, evenly spaced into the centre of
the trail and to the left and right of the main stem, lengthen
and shorten the wires throughout the whole trail, to hide
any exposed wires.

Place asparagus plumosus fern throughout the spray and
to the left and right of the main stem, softening the trail.

Cut off any excess wire to prevent the spray becoming
too bulky. Press the remaining stems firmly together and
apply Parafilm®. Grade the heights and shades of the
flowers, and repeat the design until the circlet is
completed.

Close the hook and place the flowers around the cake at
the reception.

CARE OF FRESH FLOWERS
If the flowers are required for the next morning place the
posy and circlet in a container supported by tissue paper,
lightly spray flowers and tissue with water, seal the
container. Keep in a cool position overnight.

BAUHINIAS
Spray for Top Tier of Cake

REQUIREMENTS

- 2 bauhinias
- 2 opening bauhinias
- 2 green bauhinia buds
- 4 bauhinia leaves
- 5 sprays of white dainty small flowers
- Parafilm®, green
- secateurs
- 2 hairpins, covered with Parafilm®
- tweezers
- fine paintbrush
- royal icing

STEP 1

Place an opening bauhinia into position, introduce a green bud to the left and slightly shorter than the first flower, squeeze the taped stems firmly together. Place a leaf over the main stem, introduce a small spray of white flowers slightly higher than the leaf. Place two large bauhinias into position, both facing away from you in the opposite direction slightly overlapping, now extend another two leaves behind the bauhinias at different heights and angles to each other bringing them close to the central point to hide the mechanics. Extend three sprays of white flowers evenly spaced to the left and right of the bauhinias. (At this point commence bringing the flowers and leaves in the opposite direction back over the thumb.) Place a green bud into position, extend another opening bauhinia to the right of this back over the thumb bringing them at different heights and angles to each other still coming from a central point, squeeze and tape the stems. Shorten the handle to 2.5 cm (1 in) in length and Parafilm® only exposed wires.

STEP 2

To attach the spray to the cake; position the spray, flowing over the side of the cake, using long tweezers, bend the spray to take the curve of the cake, secure the spray firmly using tweezers and the two hairpins, attach the spray onto the cake. Using a fine paintbrush and watered-down royal icing fill any holes in the cake.

Note: Advise the customer to remove the hairpins before cutting the cake.

Spray for Bottom Tier of Cake

REQUIREMENTS

- 2 large bauhinias
- 2 opening bauhinias
- 2 green bauhinia buds
- 3 leaves
- 3 sprays of small dainty white flowers
- Parafilm®, green
- hairpin
- secateurs

STEP 1

Extend three leaves in the shape of a triangle, from a central point, squeeze the taped stems firmly together, introduce another leaf in the centre of these, slightly higher than the other three placements. Position two bauhinias at different angles to each other into the centre of the spray, squeeze the stems firmly together – Parafilm® if necessary. Place three sprays of small, white flowers between the large bauhinias to soften the arrangement and hide any gaps.

Extend another two buds to the left and right of the two bauhinias, bringing them at different lengths to each other. Squeeze and tape the stems firmly together, cut off the handle to measure 2.5 cm (1 in) in length, Parafilm® any exposed wires, attach the spray to the right of the cake using a long pair of tweezers and a hairpin. Using a paintbrush and watered-down royal icing to fill any holes in the fondant.

Note: Advise the customer to remove the hairpins from the cake before cutting.

PHALAENOPSIS ORCHID
Assembling the Flower

PATTERN

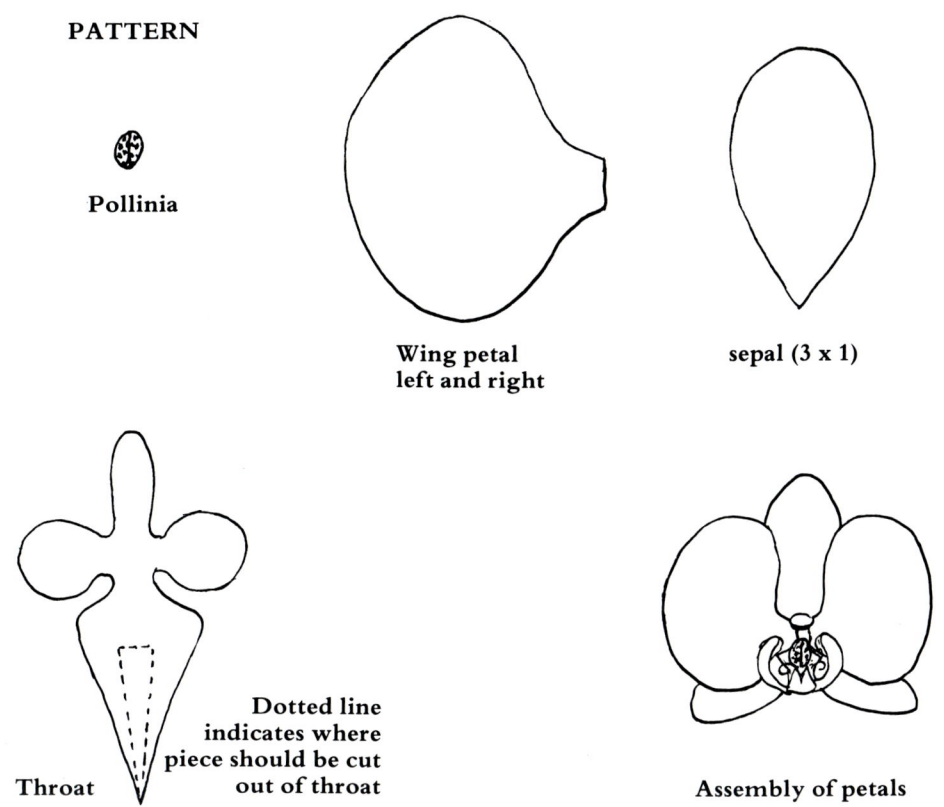

Pollinia

Wing petal
left and right

sepal (3 x 1)

Throat

Dotted line
indicates where
piece should be cut
out of throat

Assembly of petals

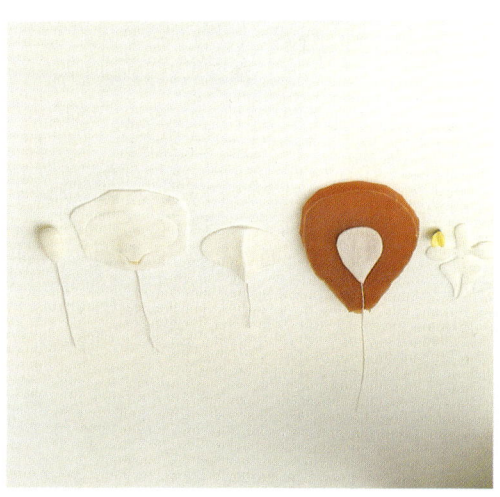

STEP 1

Mould a small log with white modelling paste, dip a fine wire into egg white and place it into the log, roll the edges thin leaving the base thick, secure the wire.

Using a medium frangipani cutter, cut out a petal, thin out and place into a latex orchid mould or roll it with a corn husk glued to a skewer, fold a line through the centre, make two more identical petals.

Make two wing petals using the same method.

Mould lemon paste into a small oval, place a knife through the centre, pressing against each side, bring up towards the centre, dot red (pollinia).

Roll paste thin and cut a throat, cut a piece out at the base using a sharp vegetable knife.

STEP 2

Using chalk, colour the base of two lobes and points of the throat lemon. Place the throat into the palm of the hand, using a ball tool, thin and cup the two lobes and bring them up towards the centre, also roll the ball tool into the two v's to bring them up towards the centre. Place into an ice ball tray for five minutes, dip wire into egg white and press into the back of the throat and leave to dry.

STEP 3

Roll out white modelling paste and using a small teardrop cutter cut out a small piece at the top, attach it with egg white to the back to cover where the wire is showing.

After moulding the wings and petals, place into a round macrame ring to dry, placing them into the position they will be wired together.

Attach the small pollinia between the two v's, paint veins at the top of the lobes and in the centre of the throat in a burgundy food colour.

STEP 4

Using a pair of tweezers, bend the wire of the throat down place the petals at 12 o'clock, 4 o'clock and 8 o'clock. Parafilm® them together, introduce the wing petals to the left and right of these, secure with Parafilm®.

Place the throat in the centre and Parafilm® all the wires together.

Make a bud in light green, mark in grooves and attach a wire.

Phalaenopsis Bud

STEP 1
Dust fingertips lightly with cornflour. Take a piece of modelling paste and mould it into the shape of a large cone. Attach it to a firm hooked wire dipped in egg white, rolling the paste at the base of the bud to form a long tail.

STEP 2
Using a sharp vegetable knife, mark five equal grooves from the top of the bud to the base. Gently bend the bud to form a slight curve.

When dry dust the bud with grated green non-toxic chalk and cornflour.

Variegated Ivy

STEP 1
Make a small sausage shape out of cream modelling paste, dip the wire into egg white and insert it into the shape. Secure the wire and roll out the paste, leaving the base thicker than the rest of the paste. Using an ivy leaf cutter or cardboard template cut out a leaf. Press it firmly into a leaf mould or mark in the veins with the back of a knife. Shape the leaf and leave it to dry over a piece of cotton wool. Paint the leaf using leaf-green food colour and methylated spirits, leaving some areas cream.

Maidenhair Fern

STEP 1
Take a stem of dried maidenhair fern, remove the foliage and secure the stem to a fine wire.

Place the fern onto a piece of greaseproof paper, press out pieces of leaf-green modelling paste between your fingers. Using a blade, mark one or two grooves at the top of the petal, press it out again, attach to the dried stem with egg white, pressing firmly to the stem to secure. Continue making the fern until completed, peel off the paper and paint the fern with leaf- green food colour and methylated spirits. Dust a small amount of brown chalk around the edge of the petal.

Hyacinth

STEP 1

Take a small amount of white modelling paste and mould it into a small Mexican hat shape. Place the calyx into a hole in a ruler and using a hyacinth cutter, cut out the flower.

Hollow out the centre of the flower with a toothpick, mark out lines in the centre of each petal.

STEP 2

Thin out the edges of each petal by pressing it firmly between two fingers, turning back each petal, bringing the petals back towards the centre.

Place a hooked wire into some egg white and bring it firmly through the centre of the flower.

Dust the dry flowers and buds with non-toxic chalks and cornflour, arrange the flowers singly or two buds and three flowers in a small spray.

Non-descript Blossom – Six Petal

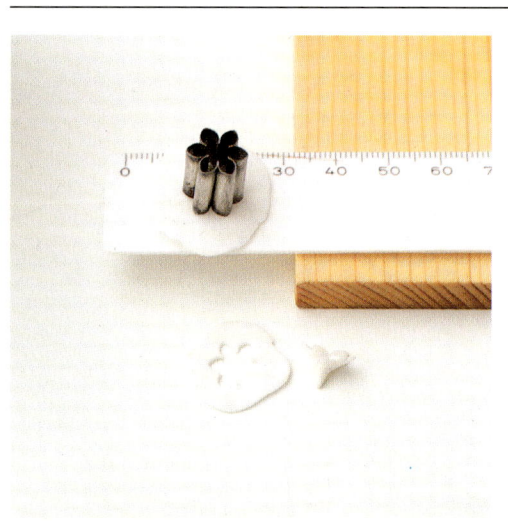

STEP 1

Mould a small Mexican hat from white modelling paste, place the calyx into the hole in a ruler and using a six-petal cutter, cut out a flower.

Use a toothpick to hollow out the centre, take a ball tool and roll it from the centre out to the tip of the petals, bringing the petals up towards the centre, place a hooked wire into some egg white and bring it firmly through the centre of the flower.

Dust the centre with pale green chalk and two petals in a light pastel chalk.

PHALAENOPSIS ORCHIDS
Spray for Top Tier of Cake

REQUIREMENTS
- 3 phalaenopsis orchids
- 4 phalaenopsis buds
- 13 leaves – frame of ivy
- 3 sprigs of maidenhair fern
- 3 sprays of hyacinths
  (3 flowers and 2 buds)
- sprays of non-descript blossom
  (5 flowers and 2 buds)

(see pp. 23-26 for flower assembly)
- Parafilm®
- secateurs
- hairpin
- long fine tweezers
- paintbrush
- royal icing

STEP 1
Make a frame of leaves (see diagram on p. 76) extend three phalaenopsis orchids into the centre of the frame, placing them at different heights and angles to each other. Extend two orchid buds from a central point, to the left and right of the phalaenopsis orchids in the centre, bringing the second bud slightly shorter and to the left of the main stem, squeeze the main stems firmly together, place a spray of hyacinths to the right of the orchid bud and a spray of blossom over the main stem to hide the mechanics.

STEP 2
Extend three sprigs of maidenhair fern from a central point, in the shape of a triangle, into the arrangement, slightly higher than the leaves.

Place two more sprays of hyacinths and blossom at varying lengths between the phalaenopsis orchids, extending them further than the line of the orchids.

STEP 3
Squeeze the taped stems firmly together, using secateurs cut the handle to about 2.5 cm (1 in) in length. Tape any exposed wires. Secure the spray to the cake using fine tweezers and a hairpin. Fill any holes in the cake with the fine paintbrush and watered-down royal icing.

Note: Advise the customer to remove the hairpins from the cake before cutting.

Spray for Bottom Tier of Cake

REQUIREMENTS

- 9 sprays of blossom flowers
- 3 sprays of hyacinths
- 4–5 maidenhair fern
- 4 phalaenopsis orchid buds

(see pp. 23–26 for flower assembly)

- opening orchid bud
- 2 phalaenopsis orchids
- 12 leaves

STEP 1

Prepare the fern and flowers with suitable wire and Parafilm® as described in top tier. (See Frame of Leaves diagram on p. 76)

STEP 2

Make a frame of leaves slightly longer and narrower than the frame required for the top tier.

Extend two phalaenopsis buds, slightly longer than the leaves from a central point, squeeze the taped stems firmly together, position a spray of blossom slightly shorter than the buds and to the right of the main stem forming a trail. Place an opening phalaenopsis bud over the main stem to hide the mechanics. Extend three sprays of hyacinths and blossom to the left and right of the trail.

STEP 3

Place two phalaenopsis orchids into the spray, bringing them over the thumb towards you one of the orchids slightly lower and at different angles to the other one. Tuck a small sprig of maidenhair fern close to the left and right of the main stem still coming from the central point. Squeeze the taped stems firmly together and Parafilm®.

Introduce three more sprays of blossom bringing them back over the thumb to the left and right of the central point. Tuck in two sprigs of maidenhair fern to the left and right of the spray. Place the remaining two buds over the thumb, and slightly lower than the other and extended longer than the leaves, press firmly against the main stem at the central point.

Cut off excess wire to form a short handle, about 1.25 cm (½ in) long and cover the remaining wire with Parafilm®.

Note: If you do not want to insert the wires into the cake, shorten the handle and attach the spray to a wooden skewer.

OPEN ROSE

STEP 1

Colour a small piece of modelling paste lightly with liquid rose-pink food colour. Sprinkle a board lightly with cornflour and using a small rolling pin, roll out the modelling paste thinly. Cut five petals using a large rose cutter. Place four of these under an airtight container. Put the remaining petal on a laminated surface, lightly dusted with cornflour. Place the index finger or thumb into a mixture of grated non-toxic chalk and cornflour and colour the top of the petal. Using a toothpick, roll back and forwards, fluting around the top edge of the petal and thinning it out at the same time.

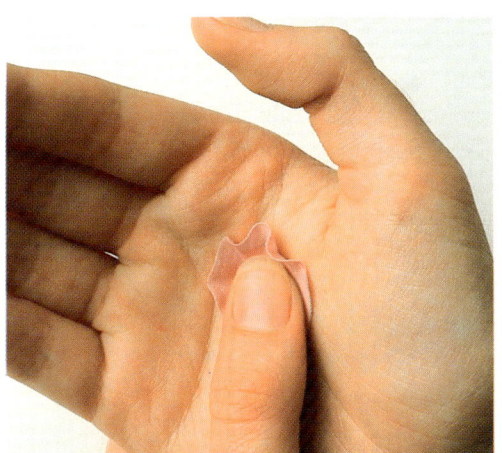

STEP 2

Dust your hands with cornflour and place the petal into the palm of your hand. Press the top three-quarters of the petal lightly and at the same time squeeze the thumb towards the centre of your hand to curve the petal. Cut out another five small rose petals and shape these in the same manner as the large petals.

STEP 3

Place a square of foil over a large macrame ring and press it into the shape of the ring. Using a No. 5 star tube, pipe a large dot of lemon royal icing into the centre of the foil. Place each of the large outside petals into the royal icing, slightly overlapping the petals. The smaller inside petals are placed, shaded side up, inside the larger petals, using a little more royal icing to attach them. They should slightly overlap each other. Tuck the last petal in at an angle.

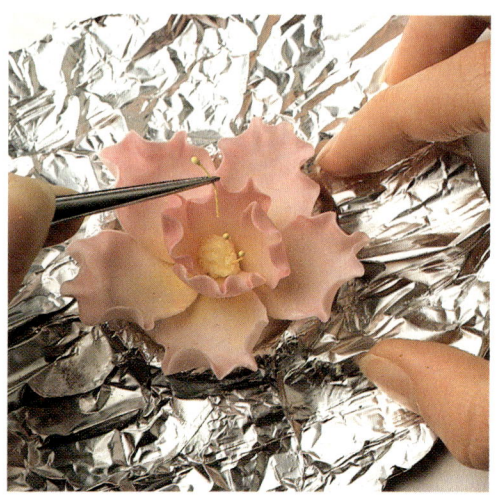

STEP 4

Cut lemon-coloured stamens to various lengths and curve them over your finger. Take a No. 5 star tube and squeeze out another dot of firm-consistency lemon royal icing in the centre of the flower. Place the stamens into position using long tweezers.

Rosebuds

STEP 1

Using a medium-sized rose cutter, cut and mould three rose petals using the same method as explained in Step 1 of Open Rose (see page 29).

STEP 2

Place firm-peak royal icing into an icing bag and using a No. 5 tube, pipe a star into the centre of a square of waxed paper.

STEP 3

Place the three dried petals into the centre of the royal icing in the shape of a triangle.

STEP 4

Now pull the waxed paper firmly up around the petals. Give the paper a slight twist and leave to dry. When dry, remove the paper.

STEP 5

Make a three-pointed calyx from leaf-green modelling paste and attach it with egg white to the bud.

Forget-me-not

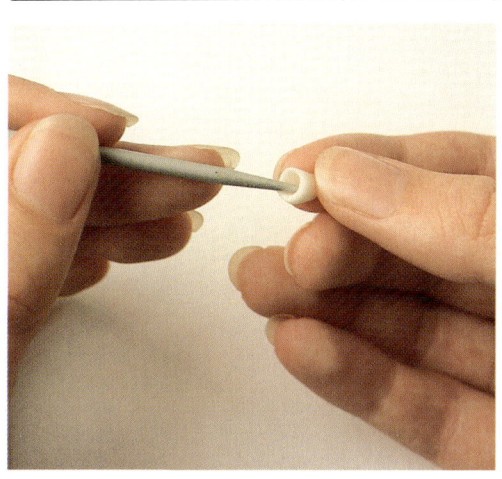

STEP 1

Dust a little cornflour onto your fingertips. Take a small piece of white modelling paste and mould it into a cone. Using a fine cable knitting needle or toothpick, hollow out the centre. Using a fine pair of pointed scissors, make 5 equal cuts.

STEP 2

Dust a little cornflour onto your fingertips and gently lift each petal out, to form a circle. Now press the first petal between the finger and thumb and gently squeeze the two sides towards the centre until the petal takes on a rounded shape. Continue in this manner until the five petals have been shaped.

STEP 3

Using a large ball tool and a stroking action, thin the petal out from the centre to the edge. Continue until the five petals have been completed. Dip a hooked wire into egg white and insert it firmly into the centre of the flower.

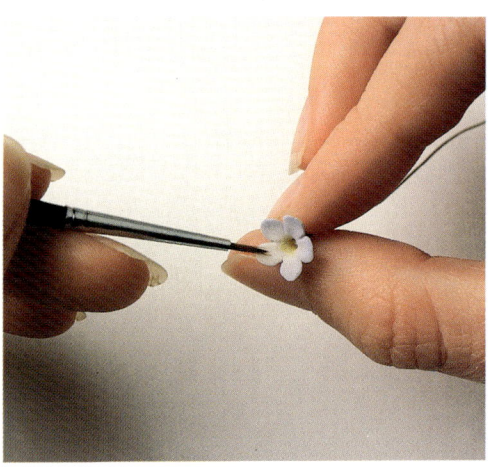

STEP 4

Paint the centre of the flower with lemon food colouring using a fine paintbrush. When dry, dust the rest of the flower with a soft blue/mauve chalk or pastel (non-toxic) mixed with a little cornflour.

Jasmine

STEP 1

Dust a small amount of cornflour onto your fingers. Take a small piece of modelling paste and mould it into the shape of a small funnel. Using a toothpick, hollow out a cone and cut this into five equal parts with scissors.

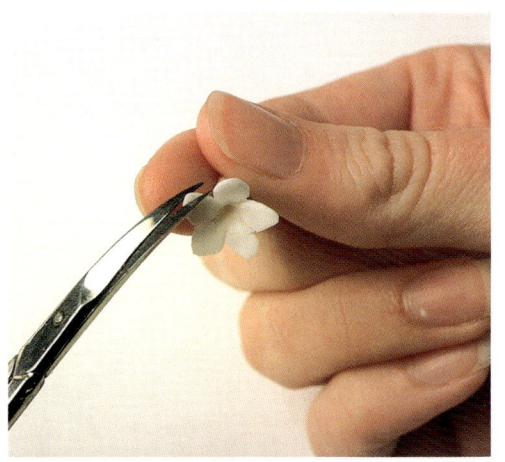

STEP 2

Press each portion firmly between the finger and thumb to thin out the petal to the required thickness. Using a pair of curved nail scissors cut two-thirds down from the centre of the petal until all the petals have been formed.

STEP 3

Using a ball tool and a stroking action, thin the petal out from the centre to the edge. Twist some of the petals so that when completed they will not appear flat.

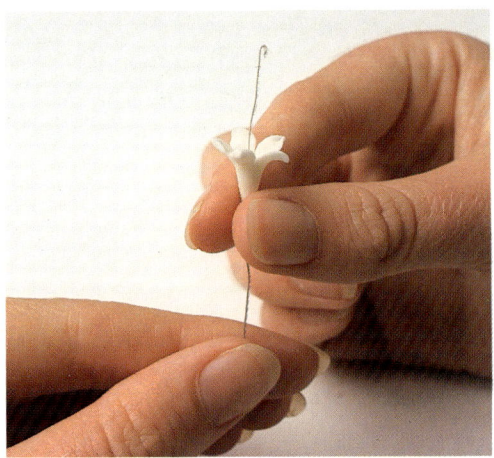

STEP 4

Dip a hooked wire into egg white and then insert it through the centre of the jasmine and secure it firmly using a pair of long tweezers. Place a small pale green stamen into the centre of the jasmine. Using leaf-green food colour, paint a small calyx at the base of the flower. When this is dry, dust or paint with rose-pink chalk of food colour the base of the trumpet, leaving the underneath petals white.

OPEN ROSES
Spray for Top Tier of Cake

REQUIREMENTS

- 4 open roses
- 4 rosebuds
- 3 sprays of jasmine
- 11 sprays of forget-me-nots
- 4 three-looped bows

(see pp. 29–32 for flower assembly)

- long tweezers
- royal icing, firm-peak consistency
- No. 5 star tube and icing bag
- No. 00 paintbrush

Note: Please advise customer wires must be taken out of cake before cutting!

STEP 1

Using a long pair of tweezers, make four holes in the centre of the cake (approximately 1.85 cm (¾ in) distance apart).

Push four sets of looped ribbons into the cake in an upright position.

Place the open roses into position at an angle, not flat, resting them against the looped ribbons, secure the first rose with a dab of royal icing underneath the petals.

Mark where the three roses will be placed on the cake, forming a circular shape. Remove them and rest them onto a piece of thin foam until ready to place into the spray.

Squeeze a small amount of royal icing under the first rosebud and centre it between the first rose and where the hole is marked for the second rose.

STEP 2

Using tweezers, insert the small sprays either side of the bud, neaten up the gaps with royal icing and a damp paintbrush.

Squeeze a small amount of royal icing under the second rose and attach it to the cake, resting it against the looped ribbons.

Attach the second rosebud between the second rose and the next hole. Join small sprays either side of this. Again neaten up the gaps with royal icing.

Using tweezers, arrange the single flowers in the centre of the cake, neatening up the holes with royal icing, placing the flowers at different heights and angles and slightly higher than the open roses.

Secure the third and fourth rose and rosebuds onto the cake, join the small sprays on either side of these buds. Neaten up the holes with royal icing.

IMPORTANT POINTS TO REMEMBER

1. Make sure the flowers are centred correctly otherwise the whole spray will be unbalanced and unsymmetrical.
2. Position the buds so that they are not aligned with the focal flowers.

3. When inserting the small sprays of flowers into the cake, place them so that they form a different line from the buds or focal flowers.

4. If the completed spray is successful, it will form a circle when viewed from above.

5. Never place this arrangement flat on a cake – always elevate the flowers.

Spray for Bottom Tier of Cake

Two sprays required for this tier. The flowers listed are for one spray.

REQUIREMENTS

- 1 open rose
- 5 small roses
- 3 sprays of jasmine
- 5 sprays of forget-me-nots
- 2 three-looped bows

(see pp. 29-32 for flower assembly)

Note: Because the wires in this spray have been placed into the cake it is imperative that the customer removes the wires from the cake before cutting it.

STEP 1

Using a pair of long-pointed tweezers, place the two three-looped bows into the cake, resting them against the centre pillar. Using a No. 5 star tube and royal icing secure the open rose, tilting it slightly, to sit against the ribbons.

Still using long tweezers, place five small roses around the open rose to form a circle. Extend a spray of jasmine to the back, left and right of the large rose.

Fill any gaps with a fine paintbrush and watered-down royal icing. Introduce five small sprays of forget-me-nots evenly throughout the spray where necessary to soften the spray and hide the mechanics.

Using a fine paintbrush and watered-down royal icing fill any holes.

Small Sprays for Top and Bottom Tiers

Sixteen sprays required for both tiers. The flowers listed are for one spray.

REQUIREMENTS

- 3 jasmine flowers
- 1 forget-me-not flower
- 1 hairpin

(see pp. 31-32 for flower assembly)

- long tweezers
- royal icing, soft-peak consistency
- No. 00 paintbrush
- long tweezers
- royal icing
- No. 5 star tube
- paintbrush

STEP 1

Wire and Parafilm® the flowers. Position three jasmine and a forget-me-not to form a circular shape, squeeze the taped stems firmly together. Cut the wires to 1.25 cm (½ in) in length. Parafilm® the remaining wires using long-pointed tweezers and a small hairpin.

STEP 2

Attach the completed spray to one corner of the cake. Fill any holes with a damp fine paintbrush and watered-down royal icing.

Continue till all 16 sprays have been attached to each corner of both tiers.

GARRETT FRILL

This frill was devised by South African decorator, Elaine Garrett.

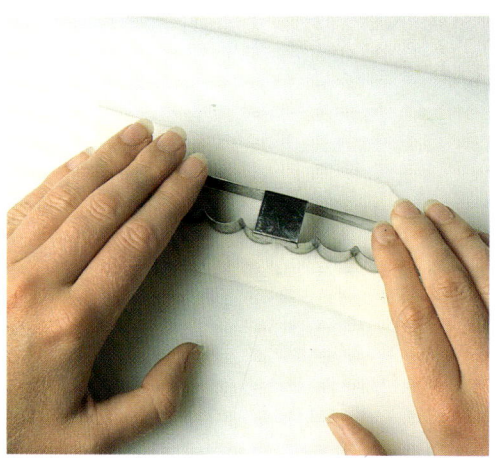

STEP 1

Knead a little sieved icing sugar into a piece of plastic fondant until the fondant is quite firm but not sticky. Sprinkle a little cornflour onto a board and thinly roll out the fondant. Using a frill cutter, cut out the frill and place it on a laminated surface which has been dusted with cornflour.

STEP 2

Press a wooden toothpick into the base of the fondant shape. Roll it backwards and forwards to form a frill, continuing in this manner until the whole piece has been completed.

STEP 3

Tuck the left hand side of the frill under, using a paintbrush dipped in egg white to attach the frill to the cake. Using a small piece of plastic acetate film, gently rub the top of the frill against the surface of the cake to eliminate any joins. Continue in this manner until the base of the cake is surrounded with the frill. Lift the frill up with a toothpick to soften the flounce.

STEP 4

Make small posies of forget-me-nots, jasmine and leaves and attach one to each corner of the cake with a small hairpin of wire, covered with green plastic florist tape. Use tweezers to do this.

Note: Plastic acetate film is available from stationery shops.

ROSE SPRAY

REQUIREMENTS
- 5 or 6 roses
- 6 or 7 rosebuds
- 7 leaves
- 5 hyacinths
- 3 sprays abelias or small flowers, each with 3 flowers and 2 buds
(see pp. 26, 29-30 for flower assembly)
- 3 sprays abelias or small flowers, each with 5 flowers and 2 buds
- 2 hairpins, covered with Parafilm®
- long tweezers

STEP 1

Position a small rosebud, then on either side of the main stem introduce two more rosebuds slightly lower than each other.

At the base of the rosebuds place a leaf to cover the wires, then place two more rosebuds on either side of this leaf slightly lower than each other forming a triangle.

Extend two hyacinths at different heights between the two rosebuds above the main stem.

Cut off excess wires and press the stems firmly together.

STEP 2

Extend two small sprays of abelias slightly lower on either side of this main stem.

Tuck a small leaf under the flowers, still forming a triangle, introducing the flowers at different lengths so that when the spray is completed the flowers will not be in alignment with each other.

Position a small leaf to the left of the spray, and, another leaf to the right of the spray. Introduce a small rosebud to the right of the main stem and a semi-open rose slightly higher into the spray.

Close to the main stem tuck a bow, to hide the mechanics and soften the spray.

Continue to form a triangle, extend two larger leaves slightly lower and to the left and right of the spray. Introduce two large sprays of abelias to the left and right of the main stem, extending them slightly higher into the focal area.

Extend a rose into the centre and recess another rose to the right of the spray.

STEP 3

Tuck another bow close to the stem, to the left of the flowers. Elevate a small spray of abelias and recess three hyacinths over the main stem, to hide any wires showing.

Squeeze the remaining wires firmly together cut off any excess wires. Stretch Parafilm® around the main stem if difficult to handle.

At this point start bringing the flowers and leaves down at right angles to the spray, taking them over the thumb in the opposite direction from before.

To the right of the focal area position another rose and tuck a large spray of abelias under the rose.

To the left and right of the main stem, place two more roses, still bringing the work towards you from a central point.

Cut the main stem to a length of 2.5 cm (1 in) to form a small handle and apply Parafilm® to the remaining wires.

Apply Parafilm® to a thick silk covered wire and cut two lengths a few centimetres long. Curve these to the shape of a hairpin. Using tweezers and the two hairpins, attach the spray to the cake.

Note: Advise customer hairpins are to be removed from cake before cutting.

SMALL ROSE SPRAY

REQUIREMENTS

- 4 small leaves
- 4 small rose buds
- 1 open rose
- 2 small flowers

(see pp. 29–30 for flower assembly)

- small hairpin, covered with Parafilm®
- Parafilm®
- long fine tweezers

STEP 1

Parafilm the wires, hook and place the flowers and leaves onto these. Place four small leaves into position from a central point, extend four small rose buds at different lengths and angles to each other, squeeze the wires firmly together.

Centre an open rose into the middle of the spray, recess two small flowers under the rose to hide the mechanics. Cut off excess wires to form a short handle and cover the remaining wires with Parafilm®

STEP 2

Using a darning needle, make two holes in the fondant where the hairpin will be placed, press the spray into position against the cake and using a long, fine pair of tweezers, secure the spray with the hairpin. Fill any holes with watered–down royal icing and a paintbrush.

Note: The spray rests against the base of the cake, it is not pushed into the plastic icing, but secured with a wired hairpin. If a hairpin is used, advise the customer to remove it from the cake before cutting.

FLOODWORK LESSON
Birthday Cake

Sketch for Birthday Cake Floodwork

REQUIREMENTS
- HB pencil
- 6H pencil
- tracing or greaseproof paper
- non-toxic blue and green chalks
- cornflour
- liquid food colours – rose pink, brown, leaf-green, black
- No. 00 paintbrush
- small laminated board
- cover – e.g. cup (to cover royal icing while painting with sugar)
- Royal icing
- small piece of foam
- knife or spatula
- water
- sable make-up brush
- mural of rabbit and mouse

STEP 1
With an extremely sharp HB pencil, trace the drawing onto tracing paper, turn the sketch over and retrace the sketch on the other side of the paper, making sure the lead does not smudge.

Turn the drawing back to the right side, so that the completed drawing is now facing you. Place the greaseproof paper onto the cake and trace the drawing lightly onto the prepared surface.

Using a 6 H pencil, draw in a light background before commencing to paint. (Take a thin piece of foam to rest your hand on while working on the cake, to prevent the sweat from your fingers getting onto the cake.)

Using green and blue chalk mixed with cornflour for the grass and sky, dust in a light background. (Apply this with a sable make-up brush.)

With liquid food colours and a firm fine paintbrush, paint in the background mural. Let the work dry before continuing.

STEP 2
Using freshly made royal icing, water and food colours, thin down the royal icing until it will spread without difficulty. Prick any air bubbles with a fine pin. Draw a line to see if you have the right consistency, place a small amount of watered-down royal icing onto it, if you can see the line the royal icing is too thin. If the icing will not spread easily, add more water or food colour to the royal icing before continuing. Be very sparing with the food colour until you have the right shade required, mix the colours on a flat board in a stroking-action to prevent air bubbles. At this stage it is necessary to examine the sketch of the rabbit and the mouse to decide which section is the furthest away to commence painting to obtain a three-dimensional effect.

STEP 3
Paint the arm and the leg of the rabbit with a fine paintbrush and watered-down royal icing, allow a few minutes for the work to develop a crust. Flood the rabbit's tail in white royal icing.

Note: Keep the watered-down royal icing covered when not in use.

Paint the inside of the rabbit's ear in pale pink royal icing, when dry paint the outside ears in white royal icing, using a stroking action and a damp paintbrush pull up fine hairs, allow a crust to form (this will take a few minutes) before continuing to paint the rabbit.

Paint the rest of the body, including the arm and the left foot in while royal icing, prick any air bubbles, allow the body to completely dry, repaint in white royal icing the left hind leg and paw and the rabbit's left arm, allow the work to dry.

Flood the face of the rabbit in white royal icing, using a damp paintbrush, in a stroking action, again pull up hairs around the face.

Repaint the inside of the sole of the paw in pale pink royal icing. When dry, paint the outside of the paw in white royal icing. Place a small pink dot in the centre of the face for a nose.

STEP 4

Using pale pink royal icing, paint the stalk of the mushroom, allow to dry. Paint underneath the mushroom with the same colour, introduce a small amount of white royal icing into this, bringing the brush back and forwards in a stroking action, to give the work light and shade.

Paint the mouse's tail brown.

Using a pale beige-coloured royal icing, paint the inside of the mouse's ears, leave to dry.

Paint the outside of the mouse's ears in brown royal icing, return to the mushroom and using a stroking action, bring the royal icing around the lower edge of the left and right side, bringing the brush underneath the mushroom. Drop in dots of white royal icing evenly spaced to form white spots, prick any air bubbles with a pin.

Using brown royal icing paint the left and right leg of the mouse, allow to dry. Paint the body in brown and introduce white royal icing, stroking the two colours together (so a line does not form where the two colours meet). Using brown and white royal icing, paint the face, when dry place a small brown nose in the centre of his face. Allow the floodwork to completely dry and paint in a small flute in brown food colour, when dry colour this silver.

Paint in the facial details with liquid food colours and a No. 00 fine paintbrush.

DRUMMER BOY
Floodwork

REQUIREMENTS

- iced white cake (iced several days) *or* white plaque
- royal icing, soft-peak consistency
- container to cover royal icing on the board
- liquid food colours: leaf-green, pillar-box red, brown, black, skin colour, lemon yellow
- green non-toxic chalk and cornflour mixture
- fine paintbrush
- thick paintbrush
- water
- laminated board
- flat knife
- tracing paper
- H.B. pencil
- 6H pencil
- thin foam (if painting straight onto cake)
- No. 00 tube and piping bag
- 2 holly leaves and 3 red berries

**Sketch for
Drummer Boy Floodwork**

STEP 1

Select a design and with an extremely sharp HB pencil, trace the selected drawing onto tracing paper. Turn the tracing over and retrace the sketch on the other side of the paper.

Turn the sketch back to the right side so that the completed drawing is now facing you.

Place the tracing paper onto the cake or plaque and trace the drawing lightly onto the prepared surface. Using a sable brush, dust green non-toxic chalk and cornflour around the outside edge of the sketch.

STEP 2

Using liquid food colour, water and freshly made royal icing mix until it will spread without difficulty. Cover until ready to use.

Prick any air bubbles with a pin. If thinning down a strong colour do not use water, just the colour. Study the sketch and decide which section is the furtherest point. Using a fine paintbrush and watered-down royal icing, begin painting. Allow a crust to form before painting the section. Continue until all the picture has been completed.

Using a fine paintbrush paint in the finer details.

Note: Keep royal icing covered as you work.

STEP 3

Roll out leaf-green modelling paste and using a small holly cutter mould two holly leaves.

Mark in veins and shape the leaves over cotton wool to dry. Colour the dry leaves with a mixture of leaf-green and methylated spirits. Make small berries when dry colour with pillar-box red and methylated spirits.

Using firm royal icing and an icing bag and a No. 1 tube secure the leaves and berries to the hat. Place cotton wool under the leaves until dry.

SPECIAL OCCASION CAKES

FRESH FLOWERS
Wedding Cake

REQUIREMENTS

- small and large round cakes, iced white
- 2 round boards, 2.5 cm (1 in) and 7.5 cm (3 in) larger than the cakes, covered with silver paper
- 3 glass pillars
- template of embroidery pattern
- darning needle
- thin white ribbon and small bows
- No. 00 and 2 writing tubes and icing bag
- piped birds
- royal icing, medium-peak consistency
- frill cutter
- extra plastic icing
- toothpick
- cornflour
- egg white
- 2 wires, size 22 (.71)
- small spray of flowers
- trail of flowers for larger cake
- miniature spray
- 2 hairpins
- Parafilm®
(see pp. 19–20 spray assembly)

Two tiers:
30 x 15 cm (12 x 6 in)
25 x 15 cm (10 x 6 in)

Three tiers:
30 x 22 x 15 cm (12 x 9 x 6 in)
25 x 20 x 15 cm (10 x 8 x 6 in)
23 x 18 x 13 cm (9 x 7 x 5 in)

The cake displayed in the photograph was cooked in round tins but oval tins could also be used. It would be pleasing to the eye to have tier cakes of the similar shape. The bottom tin should be deeper than the top one. Below are recommended sizes for making tier cakes.

Note: Glass pillars have been placed into this cake instead of plastic pillars as a variation.

To judge how much marzipan or fondant is required to cover a cake, weigh the fruit cake and halve the weight. For example, a 5 kg (10 lb) cake will require 2.5 kg (5 lb) fondant or marzipan.

STEP 1

Measure the circumference around the base of the bottom cake using a string or a piece of ribbon. Allow two 22 (.71) wires together to obtain the required length. Parafilm® these, stretching the tape until it is very thin and twist it firmly around the wires.

Using a No. 00 writing tube and medium-peak royal icing pipe a snail trail around the edge of the large cake. Close the hook and secure the two wires.

STEP 2

Hook both ends of the wires closing one of the hooks and leave the other one slightly open. Extend the focal and selected flowers and leaves to the centre wire to form a trail. Mark out where the ribbons will be placed using a darning needle and a piece of straight cardboard.

Using a greaseproof template and a darning needle, centre the embroidery pattern on both cakes. Using a No. 00 writing tube and medium-peak royal icing pipe the design. Make a Garret frill (see page 36) and place it around the base of the top tier, attaching it with egg white.

Place the three glass pillars into the cake, evenly spaced in the centre of the large cake to support the top tier. Attach the ribbons and bows to the cake.

STEP 3

Using a No. 2 writing tube and medium-peak royal icing assemble the bodies of the birds on the side of the small and large cakes, embroider a design between these to soften the effect.

When ready to be delivered to the reception, place the trail around the base of the large cake, centre the small posy in the middle of the small cake and place the miniature spray over the join in the frill in the front of the small cake.

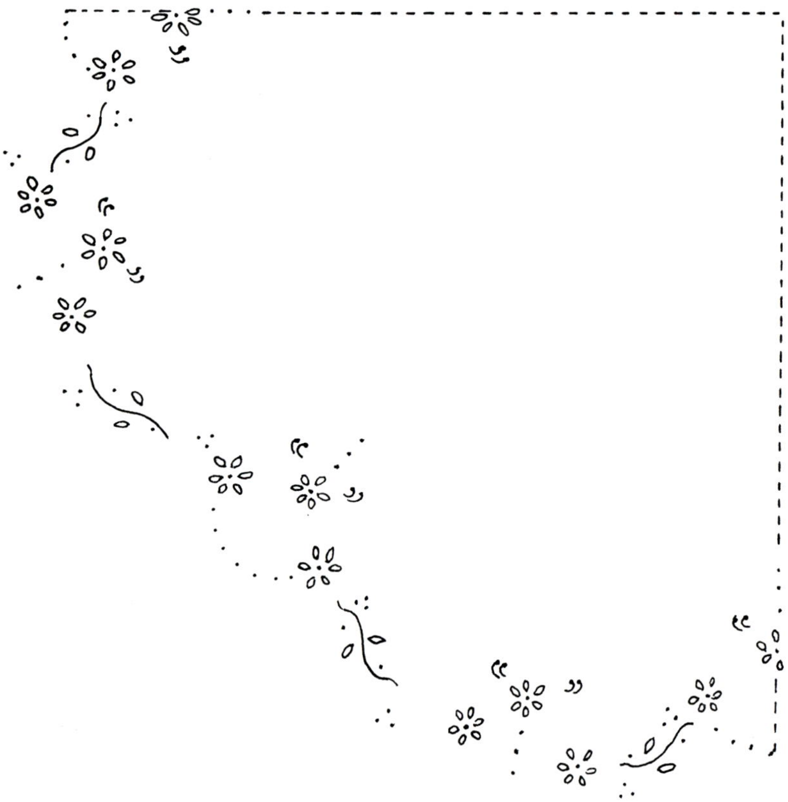

Embroidery design for top of cake – this pattern will fit a 22 cm (9 in) cake. It can be enlarged or made smaller if required

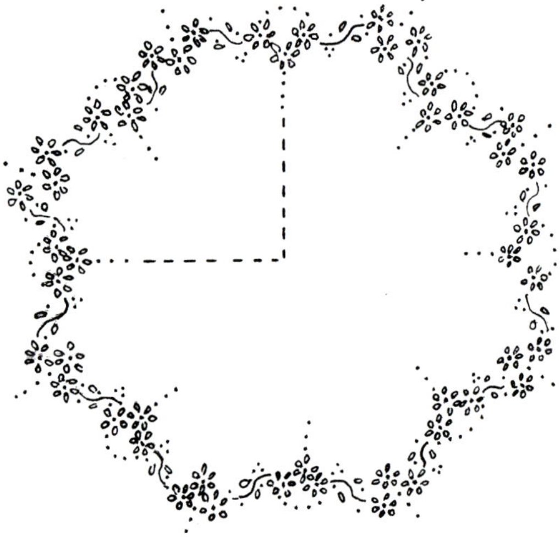

Embroidery design used with two birds

BAUHINIAS
Wedding Cake

REQUIREMENTS

- small and large scalloped oval cakes, iced white
- 2 scalloped oval boards 2.5 cm (1 in) and 5 cm (2 in) larger than the cakes, covered in silver paper
- royal icing, soft-peak and medium-peak consistency
- spray of bauhinias, for top tier
- spray of bauhinias, for bottom tier
- 3 wooden butcher's skewers
- pen
- sharp knife

(see pp. 21-22 for spray assembly)

- 2 hairpins covered with Parafilm®
- long tweezers
- Nos 00, 0 and 2 writing tubes
- sheet of photo album
- graph paper
- piped lace
- inside of a roll of masking or sticky tape
- silver paper
- paste
- strip of broderie anglaise material
- cable needle or toothpick
- scissors, pins

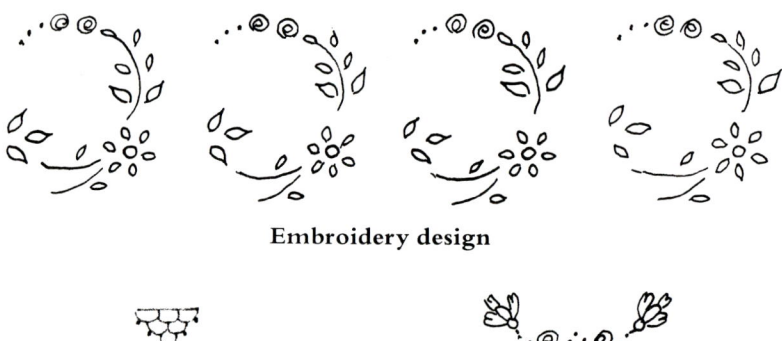

Embroidery design

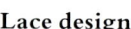

Lace design

STEP 1

Take an empty cardboard ring from the centre of a reel of sticky tape, using paste attach silver paper to the outside and a small strip around the inside of the ring.

Mark out using a ruler and darning needle, where the lace will be attached, at the base of the cake.

Using graph paper and a sheet of a photo album, and a No. 00 writing tube and soft-peak white royal icing, make piped lace and birds wings and tails (p. 51).

Using soft-peak royal icing and a No. 0 tube, pipe a snail trail around the bottom edge of both cakes.

STEP 2

Pipe wings and tails onto a sheet of photo album using a No. 00 writing tube and medium-peak royal icing. Place a piece of broderie anglaise material onto the cake, secure it with a pin and using a cable needle, mark out the eyelet holes into the cakes.

Using a No. 00 writing tube, pipe the embroidery until the design has been transferred onto the cake. Attach the lace to the two cakes with medium-peak royal icing and a No. 00 writing tube.

STEP 3

Place the covered ring into the centre of the cake, push a wooden skewer into the cake, bring it out so that the point of the skewer is facing upwards, mark a line slightly higher than the round ring, using a sharp knife cut the skewer where the line is. Attach two more pillars evenly spaced, in a triangle, resting them against the round ring. Cut these off in the same manner.

Assemble the birds onto the cake using a No. 2 writing tube for the bodies.

STEP 4

Using long tweezers and hairpins attach the wired spray to the right hand side of the bottom tier. Still using long tweezers, drape the other spray to fall softly over the side of the cake, attach it to the cake with two hairpins to hold it firmly.

Note: Advise the customer to remove the hairpins, before cutting the cake.

PHALAENOPSIS ORCHIDS
Wedding Cake

REQUIREMENTS

- small and medium-sized scalloped oval cakes, iced white
- 2 scalloped oval boards, 5 cm (2 in) and 10 cm (4 in) larger than the cakes, covered with silver paper
- Nos 00 and 2 writing tubes
- piping bag
- lemon stamens
- royal icing, soft-peak consistency

(see pp. 23–28 for flower and spray assembly)

- long tweezers
- piped lace
- darning needle and ruler
- greaseproof template
- 2 sprays of phalaenopsis orchids
- 3 hairpins (optional)
- 3 small pillars
- 3 wooden skewers

STEP 1

Attach the sprays of flowers to the top of the small cake with royal icing or a hairpin. Using a No. 00 writing tube and soft-peak royal icing, pipe a snail trail around the lower edge of the cake. Using a needle and a ruler mark out where the lace will be placed on both cakes.

Make a template in greaseproof paper of the outside edge of the cake. Draw the embroidery design and using a darning needle mark out the main points on the cake.

STEP 2

Using tweezers place small lemon stamens into the centre of the embroidery design – if stamens are not required pipe lemon dots.

Continue the embroidery design still using a No. 00 writing tube and soft-peak royal icing until the embroidery is completed. Make lace and attach it to the cake.

Piped bird

Pipe two wings and a tail   **Pipe a body and attach the tail and wings**   **Lace design**

STEP 3

Attach the pillars to the large cake, place the spray on the left hand side of the cake, draping the flowers over the side, using two hairpins to hold the flowers in place. Pipe a snail trail around the base of the cake using a No. 00 writing tube and soft-peak royal icing. Continue piping the embroidery until completed. Attach the rest of the lace and assemble two birds onto the cake using royal icing and a No. 2 writing tube.

OPEN ROSES
Wedding Cake

REQUIREMENTS

- small and large hexagonal cakes, iced white
- 2 hexagonal boards 5 cm (2 in) and 10 cm (4 in) larger than the cakes, covered with silver paper
- 4 piped birds (p. 51)
- cable needle
- No. 00 writing tube and piping bag
- long tweezers
- 16 small hairpins

(see pp. 29-36 for flower and spray assembly)

- royal icing, soft-peak consistency
- 4 small pillars
- greaseproof template
- needle
- round spray for top of cake
- 2 smaller sprays for the back and front of the bottom tier
- 16 small sprays for corners of both tiers

STEP 1

Make a template from greaseproof paper, approximately half the height of the cake and the length of one of the sides. Draw the design onto the greaseproof template in pencil. Using a pin, prick the main points, e.g. eyelet work and the centres of the flowers.

Make soft-peak royal icing, using a fine cable needle, mark out eyelet work. With royal icing and a No. 00 writing tube, embroider the three holes, piping in a circular fashion on top of the holes.

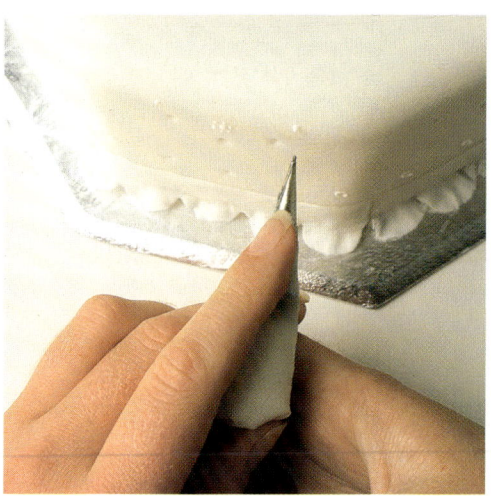

STEP 2

Pipe the centre of the flowers using a large dot for the centre and smaller dots around it to form a circle. Continue until all the centres have been piped.

Attach a 'Garrett' frill around the base of the cake. (see page 36-37)

Using a ruler and a needle, mark where the two ribbons will be placed around the cake.

STEP 3

Still using a No. 00 writing tube and soft-peak royal icing, pipe the outside petals of the flowers, curved lines and leaves. Continue this process until all the sides of the cake have been embroidered.

Attach two ribbons to the side of the cake. Embroider the eyelet holes & dots between the ribbons. Attach the small sprays of flowers on each corner of the cake.

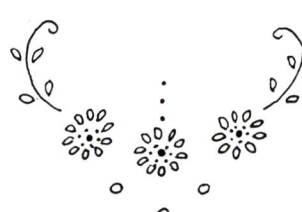

Embroidery designs

DRUMMER BOY
Christmas Cake

REQUIREMENTS

- 1 medium bell-shaped cake, iced white
- 1 bell-shaped board, 10 cm (4 in) larger than the cake, covered with silver paper
- liquid food colours: leaf-green, pillar-box red
- red ribbon
- royal icing, soft-peak and firm-peak consistency
- leaf tube and piping bag
- No. 00 writing tube
- fine paintbrush
- 2 templates
- piped lace
- darning needle
- Drummer boy sketch (p. 42)

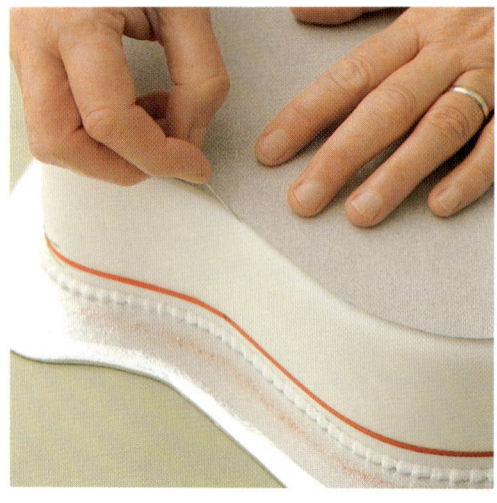

STEP 1

Make a cardboard template of the top of the cake, using a darning needle mark out the outside edge of the template. Secure a red ribbon with egg white around the bottom of the cake. Attach a lover's knot with royal icing.

Pipe a snail trail with firm-peak royal icing using a leaf tube around the base of the cake.

Place a sheet of graph paper underneath the page of a sheet of photo album paper, pipe the lace pieces using soft-peak royal icing and a No. 00 tube.

Holly leaf and berries embroidery design

STEP 2

Make a template from greaseproof paper for the embroidery at the base of the cake, half the height and the circumference of the outside of the cake. Fold the template in half until it measures approximately 2.5 cm (1 in). Mark out the main points with a darning needle. Also mark where the holly and leaves on the top of the cake will be piped.

Pipe the embroidery with a No. 00 tube and soft-peak royal icing, when dry paint the berries and leaves in pillar-box red and leaf-green, also paint the straight lines and dots at the base of the cake in the same method.

Lace design

STEP 3

Using firm-peak royal icing and a No. 00 writing tube, pipe a small line along the edge of the cake and attach the lace, using a pair of tweezers if required. (The lace must come straight out from the cake, not at an angle.)

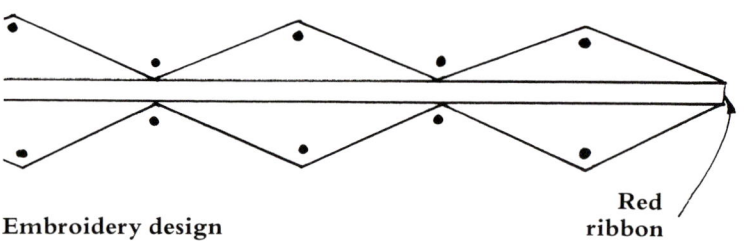

Embroidery design

Red ribbon

SCALLOPED OVAL
Birthday Cake

REQUIREMENTS

- 1 medium scalloped oval cake, iced pink
- 1 scalloped oval-shaped board, 5 cm (2 in) larger than the cake, covered in silver paper
- piped lace
- long tweezers
- hairpins covered with Parafilm®
- darning needle
- cardboard template same shape as cake
- royal icing, soft-peak consistency
- small square of thin foam
(see pp. 37-38 for spray assembly)
- cable needle
- food colours – rose-pink and green
- thin pink ribbon
- vegetable knife
- plastic icing
- round frill cutter
- plastic acetate film
- scissors, knife
- spray of small roses for base of cake
- spray of roses for top of cake (p. 39)

Lace pattern

Embroidery design

STEP 1

Using graph paper, a page of photo album, a No. 00 writing tube and icing bag, and soft-peak royal icing make piped lace. Make a template out of cardboard 1.25 cm (½ in) smaller than the top of the cake. Using a darning needle mark the outside edge of the template.

Trace the floodwork design (p. 40) using an extremely sharp HB pencil onto the cake. Pipe the name 'JOY' (p. 78) still using a No. 00 writing tube and soft-peak royal icing. Pipe the music notes. Using a mixture of cornflour and blue and green chalk dust the background in.

STEP 2

Using a darning needle mark out where the embroidery pattern will be piped. Using a No. 00 writing tube and dark pink royal icing pipe the centres of the flowers. Mark out the eyelet holes around the top of the cake, using a cable needle in this process. Pipe around the holes in a circular motion still using a No. 00 writing tube. (Use a piece of foam to rest your hand on so that the cake is not marked.)

Take a fine paintbrush and silver hobby paint, paint 'JOY' and the music notes.

Flood the mural on the top of the cake in painted sugar.

STEP 3

Continue piping the embroidery design evenly around the cake using light green and pale pink royal icing until completed. Attach the large rose spray on top of the cake using a hairpin to hold it in place (use long tweezers when doing this).

Add extra sieved icing sugar to the plastic icing, rollout the icing and using a round frill cutter or scone cutters cut out the frill, cut in half. Now using a toothpick, roll along the edge in a back and forwards action forming a frill.

Use cornflour if the icing sticks to the board. Cut small pieces of pink ribbon and insert it into the cake using a sharp vegetable knife.

Using a No. 00 writing tube, pipe a dropped scallop and dots either side of the ribbon to neaten it off. Attach the small spray to the centre of the cake with another hairpin.

★ Using a No. 00 writing tube attach the lace to top of cake.

Note: Use pencil in moderation as it has carbon in it. Indicate to the customer that there is a wire hairpin to be removed from the cake before cutting.

ROUND CHRISTENING CAKE

REQUIREMENTS

- 1 23 cm (9 in) round cake, iced white
- 1 round board, 3.75 cm (1½ in) larger than the cake, covered with silver paper
- tracing paper
- mural of lamb and baby (p. 77)
- HB pencil
- 6 H pencil
- royal icing, soft-peak and medium-peak consistency
- Nos 00 and 3 writing tubes
- sheet of photo album
- non-stick food spray
- graph paper
- liquid food colours
- non-toxic chalks – green and blue
- cornflour
- cardboard templates to mark out extension work
- greaseproof templates – top and side of cake
- darning needle or pin
- 8 small sprays of flowers
- 8 hairpins
- pair of tweezers
- No. 00 sable paintbrush

segment

**Template
(for top of cake)**

**This could be enlarged
on a photocopying machine
to fit the size of the cake**

Lace pattern

Dropped loops and dots

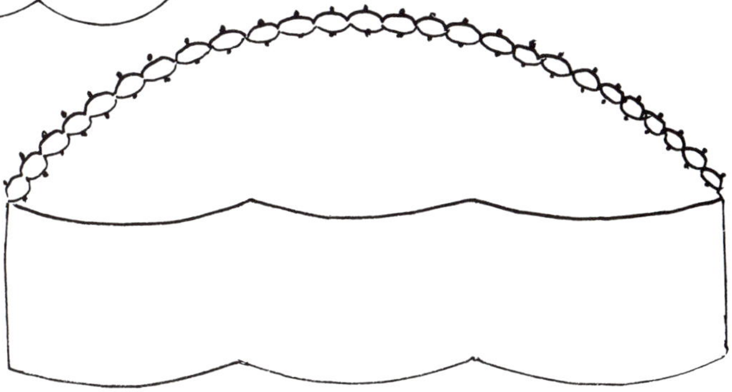

Embroidery design

Template of extension work

STEP 1

Make a template of a scalloped circle 2.5 cm (1 in) smaller than the size of the cake, place this on top of the cake and mark around the edge of the template with a darning needle or a pin. Trace the floodwork design onto the top of the cake, dust a chalk background, paint in leaves and flowers with watered-down liquid food colours. When dry, flood the mural of the lamb and the baby. Place a sheet of graph paper underneath the page of a photo album, spray it with non-stick food spray. (See Floodwork lessons on pp. 40-43.)

Using medium-peak royal icing and a No. 00 writing tube, pipe the lace required.

Pipe a small dropped loop and a dot inside the market scalloped line, using a No. 00 writing tube and soft-peak royal icing.

STEP 2

Make a template from greaseproof paper, approximately 2.5 cm (1 in) high and the circumference of the outside edge of the cake.

Fold the template so it resembles the pleats of a dress, when you have divided into eight equal parts, place it around the base of the cake, securing it to the cake with a pin, mark out the eight sections with a darning needle.

STEP 3

Remove the greaseproof template and place the cardboard template of the extension work, into the centre of these two dots, mark out where the bottom of the bridge of the extension work will form from.

Still using the needle and template, mark where the extension work will commence from.

Using a No. 00 writing tube and soft-peak royal icing, pipe the embroidery design, eight times, evenly around the top of the side of the cake.

STEP 4

Using a darning needle and the curved cardboard template, mark out a half circle to form above the extension work. Using soft-peak royal icing and a No. 00 writing tube, pipe a small dropped loop either side of the marked line, pipe a small dot on each of the scallops. Continue in this manner until all eight curves have been completed.

STEP 5

Pipe a snail trail around the base of the cake using a No. 00 writing tube and soft-peak royal icing.

Pipe the name onto the cake (resting a piece of foam onto the cake to do this) using a No. 00 writing tube and soft-peak royal icing, when dry paint the name in silver, using a fine paintbrush.

Attach the piped lace to the top of the cake with medium-peak royal icing and a No. 00 writing tube.

STEP 6

Pipe the first scallops between the dots to form a base for the extension work, using a No. 3 writing tube and firm-peak royal icing. Continue building out one scallop at a time, piping each scallop slightly shorter until four loops have been built out, make the fifth loop the same size as the first one. Continue piping around the cake until all the scallops have been completed. Allow to dry completely, before continuing.

Tilt the cake towards you, select a point and commence piping, using medium-peak royal icing and a No. 00 writing tube, pipe straight lines from the line marked to the scallops below. Place these lines firmly under the built out work at the base of the cake, neatening it off with a damp paintbrush if necessary. (It is essential to work at eye level to do this procedure.)

Attach the small sprays of flowers, between the extension work at the base of the cake, securing it with a pair of tweezers and small wired, parafilmed hairpins.

Note: Advise the customer to remove the hairpins, before cutting the cake.

SIMPLE ROUND CHRISTENING CAKE

REQUIREMENTS

- 1 23 cm (9 in) round cake, iced lemon
- 1 round board, 5 cm (2 in) larger than the cake, covered with gold paper
- spray of flowers
- hairpin, tweezers, HB pencil
- tracing paper
- fine paintbrush No. 0 or No. 00
- liquid food colours – brown, lemon, green, pink and mauve
- royal icing, soft-peak and firm-peak consistency
- piped birds on graph paper (wings and tails) (p. 51)
- Nos 5 and 8 star tubes
- Nos 00 and 1 writing tubes
- green ribbon, thick
- sharp knife
- egg white
- cable needle

STEP 1

Using a sharp knife, insert a wide green ribbon into the base of the cake. Place a pin in to secure and using egg white, attach the ribbon firmly around the bottom edge of the cake. Again using the knife, insert the end piece of the ribbon into the cake. When dry remove the pin and place a lover's knot bow over the hole in the cake, securing it to the cake with a small amount of royal icing. Using graph paper covered with plastic wrap and a No. 00 writing tube, pipe the wings and tails of the birds. Pipe a star using a No. 8 star tube and firm-peak royal icing every 3.2 cm (1¼ in) around the base of the cake. Change to a No. 5 star tube and pipe smaller stars between these, now using a No. 1 writing tube and firm-peak royal icing, pipe a dropped loop between these stars. Continue piping until the base of the cake has been completed.

STEP 2

Mark out the embroidery using a greaseproof template, using a fine cable needle make the eyelet holes into the cake where needed. Pipe the design with a No. 00 writing tube and soft-peak lemon royal icing.

Using a hairpin and long tweezers, attach the spray to the left of the top of the cake. Fill any holes with watered-down lemon royal icing and a damp paintbrush.

STEP 3

Trace the picture (p. 78) with a sharp HB pencil, turn the tracing paper over and retrace the other side of the sketch back onto the right side, place a thin piece of foam onto the cake to rest your hand and retrace the mural neatly onto the cake. With watered-down royal icing and liquid food colours, flood the design onto the cake.

Using a No. 2 writing tube pipe the bodies and beaks of the birds, using tweezers attach the wings and tails while still wet. Pipe a small embroidery design between the birds to finish off the cake.

Using a No. 00 writing tube and soft-peak royal icing pipe the name, when dry using a fine paintbrush paint the name (p. 78) in gold paint.

Eyelet Work

Embroidery design

SAILING BOAT CAKE

REQUIREMENTS

- 1 square fruit cake
- 1 cake board covered with silver paper
- cardboard template for cake (p. 80)
- cardboard template for sails (p. 80)
- marzipan
- melted chocolate
- vegetable knife
- sharp knife
- lemon, pillar-box red and sky-blue food colours
- fine paint brush
- No. 5 star tube and icing bag
- royal icing, firm-peak consistency
- plastic icing
- No. 00 writing tube

STEP 1

Place the cardboard template onto the cake, and using an electric knife (if available) cut to the shape of the template.

Ice the cake in white fondant, place onto a covered board.

Mould two pieces of red modelling paste into the shape of a long roll to fit around the front and the back end of the boat.

Using white, firm-peak royal icing and a No. 5 star tube pipe a snail trail around the base of the cake.

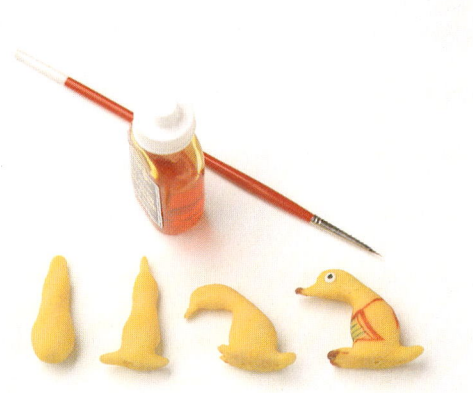

STEP 2

Using soft-peak royal icing and a No. 00 writing tube pipe the child's name onto the side of the boat. When dry paint this using a fine brush in sky-blue liquid food colour.

Using lemon marzipan and a sharp vegetable knife, mould several small ducks, dip the beaks and feet into melted chocolate and allow to dry.

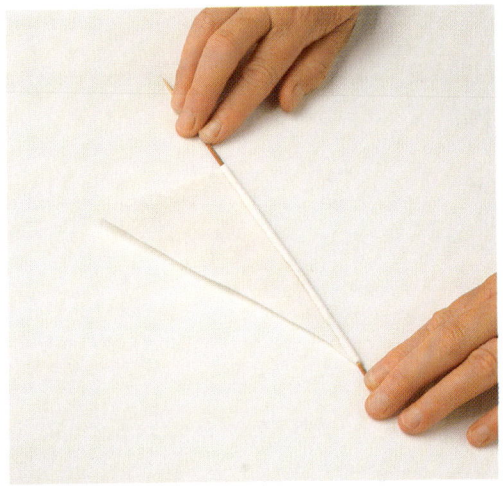

STEP 3

Make two cardboard templates for the sails and roll out white modelling paste until thin (leaving 5 cm (2 in) uncovered, to be placed into the cake) brush the edge of the sail with egg white, place the stick into position and roll it until the stick is completely covered with modelling paste, place it onto laminated board (or cotton wool if a shaped sail is required) turn frequently until dry. Make another smaller sail in the same method, when dry, place the two sails into position, pushing the skewers firmly into the cake. Pipe the name or age onto one of the sails, using a fine brush and pillar-box red food colour paint the number on the sail. Position the small animals onto the deck of the sailing boat.

GOLDEN ANNIVERSARY CAKE
Octagonal Shape

REQUIREMENTS

- 1 medium size octagonal cake, iced white
- 1 board 5 cm (2 in) larger than octagonal cake, covered with gold paper
- long tweezers
- hairpin
- embroidery template
- royal icing, soft-peak consistency
- darning needle
- olive green ribbon
- sharp vegetable knife
- egg white
- fine paintbrush
- 2 gold rings
- Parafilm®, green
- fresh, silk or sugar spray of flowers, made into a wired spray

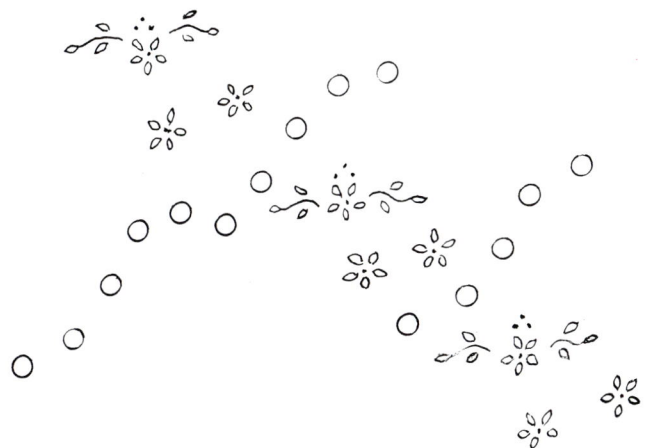

Embroidery design for side of cake

STEP 1

Using a sharp vegetable knife, make small slit into the icing, using a fine paintbrush and egg white, paint the hole, insert a pin to hold it for the time being and firmly bring the ribbon around the cake. Add additional egg white to the hole and insert the other end of the ribbon into the cake using a sharp knife to do this. Remove the pin when dry, use soft-peak royal icing to hide the hole if required.

Mark out the embroidery with a greaseproof template and a darning needle.

Using long tweezers and a hairpin, attach the spray of roses to the centre of the cake.

With a No. 00 writing tube and soft-peak royal icing, embroider the design, continue piping until the eight sides have been completed.

Attach the rings to the cake with royal icing.

Note: Because wires can be dangerous, notify the customer to remove the hairpin from the flowers before cutting the cake.

MALE CAKE
Suitable for 21st Birthday or Father's Day

REQUIREMENTS

- 1 medium size hexagonal cake, iced lemon
- 1 hexagonal board, covered with gold paper
- royal icing, soft-peak and firm-peak consistency
- tracing paper
- required mural
- HB pencil
- No. 00 writing tube
- No. 5 star tube
- fine paintbrush
- lemon, green and brown liquid food colours
- yellow, brown, green and black food pens
- board
- flat knife or spatula
- container, to cover board with
- water
- green chalk and cornflour
- sable makeup brush
- brown and green narrow ribbons
- small piece of thin foam

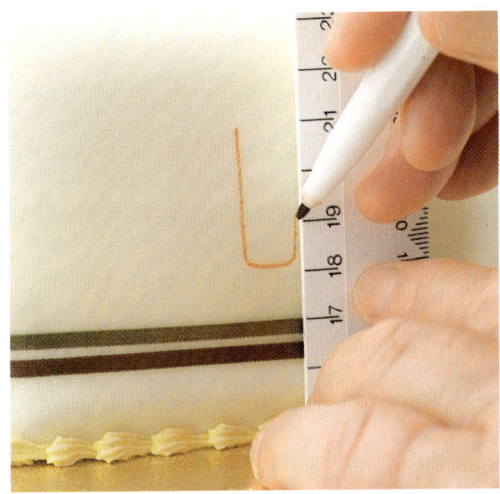

STEP 1

Place a small piece of foam onto the cake, to rest your hand on and using a HB pencil trace the mural onto the cake (see p. 42 'Drummer Boy' for floodwork details). Dust a mixture of grated, green chalk and cornflour around the edge of the mural.

Water down the royal icing with liquid food colours and water. Prick any air bubbles and cover this until ready to use.

Take a fine paintbrush and watered-down royal icing and paint the mural, commencing with the furtherest point, allowing each section to dry before continuing the next portion, prick any air bubbles.

Paint in the fine details when dry.

Using a No. 00 writing tube, pipe the name and the '21' in soft-peak royal icing, take a fine paint brush and paint the writing in gold.

Using a No. 5 star tube and a firm-peak lemon royal icing, pipe a snail trail around the base of the cake.

Attach a brown and green ribbon around the cake, attach a bow with royal icing.

Draw a beer bottle and bubbles onto the side of the cake and dust a small amount of green chalk around this. Paint the bottle with brown colour and the bubbles lemon. Colour the KB with a black food pen. Paint the leaves with a green pen. Paint the '21' in black. Complete the design with three lemon dots and a brown one. Continue until all the sides of the cake have been completed.

Embroidery

EASTER EGGS
STEP-BY-STEP CHOCOLATE EGG

STEP 1

Place chopped compound chocolate into a double boiler, stir lightly until melted, if the chocolate becomes difficult to work with, add one or two drops of white shortening to the mixture.

Note: Make sure the water in the bottom pan never boils.

STEP 2

Using a plastic egg mould, spoon the melted chocolate into one side of the mould, turn the egg around to coat the mould completely, tap it on the bench to release any air bubbles.

Place the mould into the fridge for 30 minutes until the plastic becomes foggy. When this occurs, add additional melted chocolate to the egg mould, turning it again to coat the inside of the mould.

Place it back in the fridge to set, remove it from the mould when ready.

STEP 3

Join the two chocolate halves together with melted chocolate. Attach the egg with melted chocolate to a board.

Leave until ready to decorate in a cool room. (The chocolate egg can be placed onto cotton wool if not required on a board.)

Note: Use white cotton gloves when making and decorating a chocolate egg.

DECORATED EASTER EGG
Floodwork

REQUIREMENTS

- 1 chocolate egg
- spray of wired small flowers
- tracing of rabbit and leaves attached to chocolate egg mould and covered with greaseproof paper
- royal icing, soft-peak consistency
- fine paintbrush
- small board
- liquid food colours – leaf-green, brown, lemon and black
- round board, covered with silver paper (large enough to sit the chocolate egg and leaves on)
- round board, covered with pink stretch material, 3.75 cm (1½ in) larger than the previous board
- cabbage leaves, from the inside of the cabbage
- chocolate compound
- double boiler
- extra small flowers
- piped lace
- completed chocolate leaves made from cabbage
- flooded rabbit
- egg white
- pair white gloves
- extra flooded green leaves

STEP 1

Using an HB pencil trace the rabbit and leaves (p. 79), attach it to an egg mould and cover with greaseproof paper, using tucks in the paper if necessary. Take a fine paintbrush and soft-peak royal icing and flood the picture. Allow to dry completely.

Wash and dry the inside leaves of a cabbage, paint the inside of these with melted compound chocolate and place in the fridge to set, peel the leaves off the chocolate and leave stand until ready to use. Attach the chocolate egg to the small board using melted chocolate to secure it, secure the floodwork with egg white or royal icing and using melted chocolate arrange the leaves around the egg, place thin foam or cotton wool to hold the leaves while they dry.

Attach the spray of flowers with melted chocolate between the rabbit and where the chocolate leaves form, to hide the mechanics. Place additional leaves and small flowers where necessary to complete.

Attach the piped lace with soft-peak royal icing. To complete place the egg onto the material covered board.

Note: Use white gloves and work in a cool temperature (e.g. air conditioner or a fan) when working with chocolate as it marks very easily, if this happens, reheat the chocolate in a double boiler, making sure the water does not come to the boil and re-melt the chocolate. If it is too thick add a few drops of melted white shortening.

DECORATED EASTER EGG
Flowers

REQUIREMENTS

- 12 rose leaves
- 3 roses
- 5 sprays of dainty flowers
- extra chocolate
- stand (to support egg in)
- extra spray of flowers
- Parafilm®
- white gloves

STEP 1

Secure the egg to the stand. Make a frame of leaves, place the two roses into the centre of this, positioning one slightly higher than the other, over the main stem.

Bring the third rose from a central point back over the thumb towards you, tuck in the sprays of dainty flowers to the left and right of the roses. Place the other three sprays of small flowers where necessary to balance the spray, still bringing them from a central point, squeeze the stems firmly together, cut off the main stem to a length of 2.5 cm (1 in) to form a handle and apply Parafilm® to the remaining wires.

Make a similar spray of flowers to be placed at the base of the egg for decoration.

If required pipe an edge around the egg using a No. 5 star tube and soft-peak royal icing.

Attach the spray to the easter egg with melted chocolate.

Note: When working with chocolate it is advisable to use white gloves, to prevent the chocolate from smudging.

Frame of Leaves

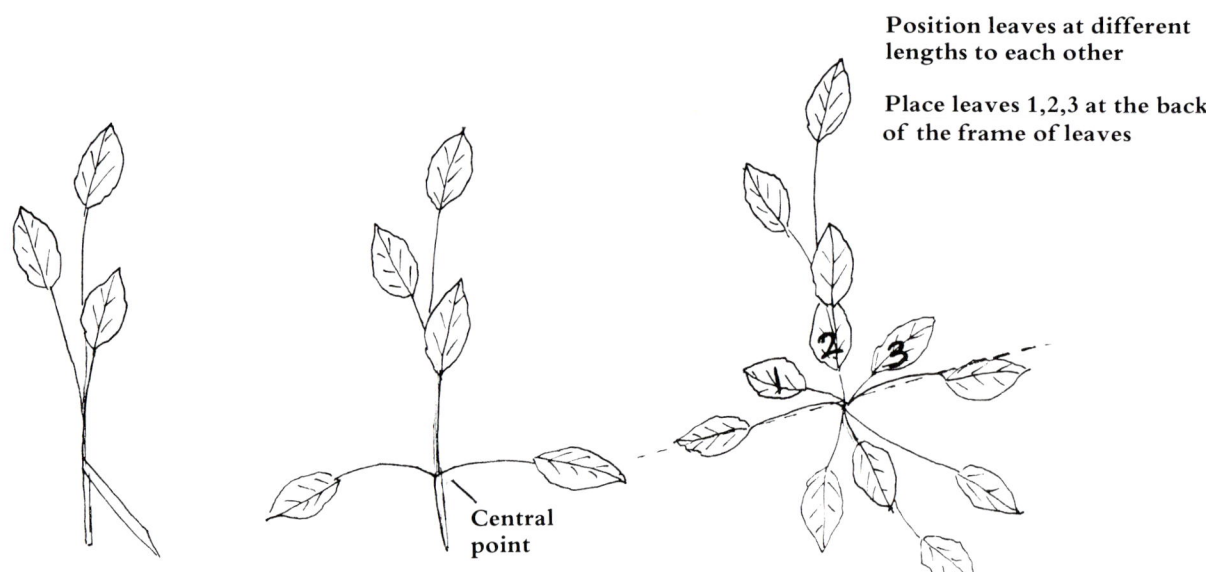

Position leaves at different lengths to each other

Place leaves 1,2,3 at the back of the frame of leaves

Central point

Position first three leaves, squeeze and Parafilm®

Position next two leaves either side of the central point

Commence bringing the work back over the thumb in the opposite direction after the central point (note dotted line)

SKETCHES

Lamb and baby – Round Christening Cake

Decorative Initials

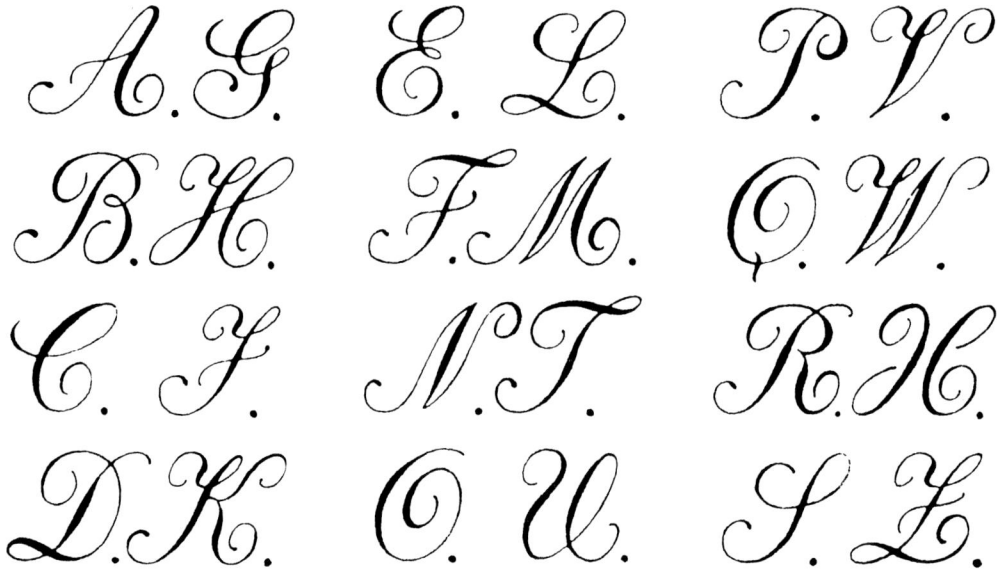

Simple Round Christening Cake

Decorated Easter Egg

Sailing Boat Cake

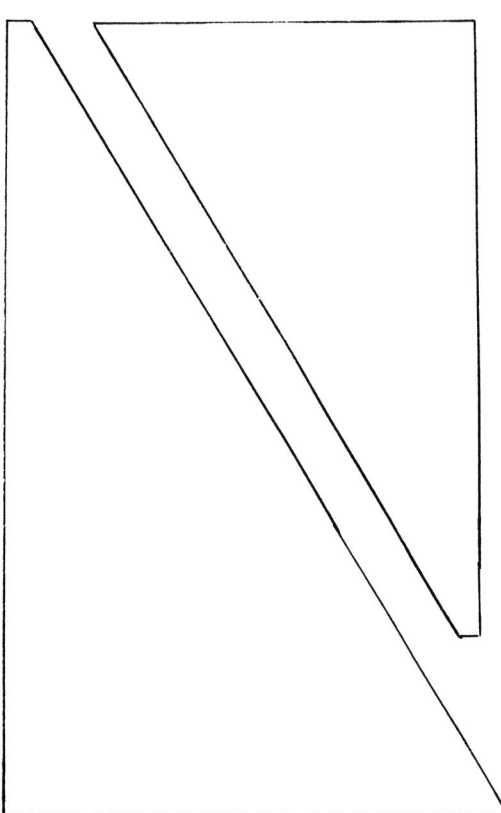

Pattern of Sails

Template of Boat